# THE WOMEN IN THE GENEALOGY OF JESUS

Demystifying the Stories of Sarah, Rebecca, Leah, Tamar, Rahab, Ruth, Bathsheba, and Mary with accompanying prayer points for modern women.

Osasohan Agbonlahor, Ph.D.

Copyright © 2024 Osasohan Agbonlahor

All rights reserved

No part of this book may be reproduced, or stored in a retrieval system, or transmitted in any form or by any means, electronic, mechanical, photocopying, recording, or otherwise, without express written permission of the publisher. Unless otherwise identified, Scriptural quotations are taken from the HOLY BIBLE, NEW KING JAMES VERSION.

Printed in the United States of America

## DEDICATION

To my beloved parents,
Barr. Victor and Mrs. Edugie Agbonlahor
You planted the seeds of faith and devotion in my heart,
nurtured them with wisdom and grace,
and watched as they blossomed into a life of purpose.
For raising me to be a woman of faith,
for showing me the power of perseverance and prayer,
and for always pointing me towards God's unfailing love,
I am eternally grateful.

# CONTENTS

Title Page
Copyright
Dedication
INTRODUCTION 1
Chapter 1: SARAH - FAITH, PATIENCE, AND GOD'S PROMISE 8
Chapter 2: REBECCA - DIVINE CONNECTIONS AND ANSWERED PRAYERS 24
Chapter 3: LEAH: The Most Unloved Wife in the Bible 42
Chapter 4: TAMAR – THE WRONGED WOMAN 64
Chapter 5: RAHAB - FROM HARLOT TO HEROINE 89
Chapter 6: RUTH – A STORY OF REDEMPTION 101
Chapter 7: BATHSHEBA - FROM SCANDAL TO ROYALTY 124
Chapter 8: MARY - A LIFE SURRENDERED TO GOD'S WILL 136
CLOSING CHAPTER: EMBRACING OUR LEGACY, LIVING OUR DESTINY 166

# INTRODUCTION

Welcome to "The Women in the Genealogy of Jesus: Demystifying the Stories of Sarah, Rebecca, Leah, Tamar, Rahab, Ruth, Bathsheba, and Mary." This book is an invitation to embark on a journey through the lives of eight extraordinary women whose stories are woven into the very fabric of our Christian faith.

As I was preparing to write this book, I found myself deeply inspired by the song "Same God" by Elevation Worship. The lyrics of this powerful song remind us that the God we serve today is the same God who moved in the lives of Jacob, Moses, Mary, and David. The words, "O God, my God, I need You / O God, my God, I need You now / How I need You now," have resonated deeply with my own heart particularly at times when I find myself in need of God's intervention and grace.

In the spirit of this beautiful song, we will embark on a journey of calling upon the God of Sarah, Rebecca, Leah, Tamar, Ruth, Rahab, Bathsheba, and Mary. As we explore their stories, we will adapt the lyrics of "Same God" to reflect the unique ways in which God moved in each of their lives. Here is my adaptation of this powerful song:

**I'm calling on the God of Sarah**
Whose promise seemed impossible to bear
You proved Your faithfulness, Your covenant endures

**I'm calling on the God of Rebecca**
Who guided the servant to find her
I trust You now to lead me to my destiny

**O God, my God, I need You**

O God, my God, I need You now
How I need You now
O Rock, O Rock of ages
I'm standing on Your faithfulness
On Your faithfulness

**I'm calling on the God of Leah**
Who saw her sorrow and opened her womb
I know with You, I'm never overlooked or forsaken

**I'm calling on the God of Tamar**
Who vindicated her when all hope was lost
I may face injustice, but You're my righteous judge

**I'm calling on the God of Ruth**
Who redeemed her life from emptiness
I cling to You, my Kinsman-Redeemer

**I'm calling on the God of Rahab**
Who saved her by a scarlet cord of faith
I once was lost, but now I'm found in You

**I'm calling on the God of Bathsheba**
Who brought forth a king from her shame
You can turn my mourning into dancing

**I'm calling on the God of Mary**
Whose womb carried the Hope of the world
Let it be to me according to Your word

**You heard these women then**
You hear Your daughters now
You are the same God
You are the same God

**You answered prayers back then**
And You will answer now
You are the same God
You are the same God

**You moved in power then**

God, move in power now
You are the same God
You are the same God

**AMEN and AMEN!**

These women, each unique in their own way, played pivotal roles in the lineage of Jesus Christ. Their lives, marked by trials, triumphs, and unwavering faith, serve as a testament to the power of God's love, grace, and redemption. By exploring their stories, we gain a deeper understanding of God's plan for His daughters and the incredible ways in which He works through the lives of ordinary women to accomplish His extraordinary purposes.

In the following chapters, we will dive into the lives of Sarah, Rebecca, Leah, Tamar, Ruth, Rahab, Bathsheba, and Mary. Each woman's story is a masterpiece of God's handiwork, showcasing His faithfulness, sovereignty, and ability to bring beauty from ashes. As we explore their journeys, we will uncover valuable lessons and insights that are just as relevant for us today as they were thousands of years ago.

Sarah's story will teach us about the power of faith and the importance of trusting in God's timing, even when His promises seem impossible. Rebecca's journey will showcase the beauty of God's providence and the significance of seeking His guidance in every decision we make. Leah's life will reveal the depths of God's love and compassion for the brokenhearted and the transformative power of His grace.

Tamar's story, though marked by heartache and injustice, will demonstrate God's ability to vindicate and restore those who have been wronged. Ruth's devotion and loyalty will inspire us to cling to God, our ultimate Redeemer, and to trust in His plan for our lives. Rahab's faith will remind us that no one is beyond the reach of God's salvation and that He can use even the most unlikely individuals for His glory.

Bathsheba's story, though born out of tragedy and sin,

will reveal the depths of God's mercy and His ability to bring redemption and purpose out of even the darkest of circumstances. And finally, Mary's life will stand as a beautiful example of surrendering to God's will, embracing the impossible, and walking in faith and obedience.

As we journey through the lives of these remarkable women, we will also have the opportunity to reflect on our own stories and the ways in which God is working in and through us. Each chapter will include powerful prayers inspired by the lives of these women, inviting us to draw near to God and to seek His face in every season of our lives.

Whether you find yourself facing daunting challenges, wrestling with persistent doubts, or grappling with overwhelming uncertainties, the transformative stories of these remarkable women will offer you unshakable hope, divine encouragement, and the soul-anchoring assurance that our God is forever faithful, unconditionally loving, and more than able to do exceedingly, abundantly above all that we could ever ask or imagine.

So, dear reader, I invite you to come and join me on this incredible journey of discovery and faith. May the extraordinary lives of Sarah, Rebecca, Leah, Tamar, Ruth, Rahab, Bathsheba, and Mary inspire you, challenge you, and deepen your understanding of God's great love and glorious purpose for your life. May their stories become beautifully interwoven with your own, as you courageously step out in faith and wholeheartedly trust in the One who holds your future securely in His loving hands.

As we embark on this life-changing journey together, I want to start with a prayer for you, dear reader:

Heavenly Father,

I come before You today, lifting up each and every precious reader who will embark on this transformative journey through the lives of these remarkable women. I pray that as they delve into the pages of this book, Your Holy Spirit would illuminate their hearts and minds, granting them fresh revelation and deep insight into Your character and Your ways.

May the stories of Sarah, Rebecca, Leah, Tamar, Ruth, Rahab, Bathsheba, and Mary come alive in new and powerful ways, speaking directly to the unique circumstances and challenges that each reader faces. I pray that every woman who reads this book would be filled with a renewed sense of hope, faith, and purpose, knowing that the same God who moved mightily in the lives of these biblical heroes is still at work today, lovingly guiding and directing their steps.

Father, I ask that You would use the truths contained within these pages to bring healing to the brokenhearted, strength to the weary, and comfort to those who mourn. May each reader experience the transformative power of Your love, grace, and redemption in new and profound ways, and may they emerge from this journey with a deeper understanding of their identity and purpose in Christ.

I pray that as they call upon the God of Sarah, Rebecca, Leah, Tamar, Ruth, Rahab, Bathsheba, and Mary, they would be filled with a renewed sense of faith and expectancy, knowing that You are able to do immeasurably more than they could ever ask or imagine. May they be inspired to step out in bold obedience and trust, knowing that You are with them every step of the way.

Thank You, Lord, for the gift of Your Word and for the powerful testimonies of these remarkable women. May their stories continue to shape and transform lives for generations to come, and may every reader who embarks on this journey be drawn ever closer to Your heart.

And Lord, I also want to lift up those readers who may not yet have a personal relationship with You. I pray that as they read these pages and encounter the transformative power of Your love and grace, they would be drawn to the foot of the cross. May they come to understand the depth of Your love for them, and the incredible sacrifice that Jesus made on their behalf.

I pray that the Holy Spirit would convict their hearts and reveal to them their need for a Savior. May they recognize that apart from Christ, they are lost and without hope, but that in Him, they can find forgiveness, redemption, and eternal life.

Father, I ask that You would give them the courage to confess their sins, to repent, and to put their faith and trust in Jesus Christ as their Lord and Savior. May they experience the joy and peace that comes from knowing You, and may they begin a lifelong journey of growing in their relationship with You.

Thank You, Lord, for Your great love and for the gift of salvation that is available to all who call upon Your name. May every reader of this book come to know You in a deep and personal way, and may their lives be forever changed by the power of Your grace. AMEN & AMEN!

I also want to extend a special invitation to those readers who may not yet have a personal relationship with You. If you find yourself longing for the hope, love, and redemption that can only be found in Christ, I want to encourage you to take a step of faith today. The Bible tells us that "if you declare with your mouth, 'Jesus is Lord,' and believe in your heart that God raised him from the dead, you will be saved" (Romans 10:9).

If you're ready to make Jesus the Lord of your life, I invite you to pray this simple prayer with me:

Dear God,

I acknowledge that I am a sinner in need of Your grace and forgiveness. I believe that Jesus Christ died on the cross for my sins and that He rose again, conquering death and offering me the gift of eternal life. Today, I choose to surrender my life to You. I confess with my mouth that Jesus is Lord, and I believe in my heart that You raised Him from the dead.

Thank You for loving me, forgiving me, and giving me a fresh start. I invite You to be the Lord of my life, and I commit to following You all the days of my life. Fill me with Your Holy Spirit and empower me to live a life that honors and glorifies You.

In Jesus' name I pray, Amen.

If you prayed that prayer, I want to congratulate you on making the most important decision of your life. Welcome to the family of God! I encourage you to find a local church where you can grow in your faith, connect with other believers, and discover the incredible plans that God has for your life.

May the God of Sarah, Rebecca, Leah, Tamar, Ruth, Rahab, Bathsheba, and Mary fill you with His peace, joy, and abiding presence as you embark on this exciting journey of faith.

Amen and Amen!!

# CHAPTER 1: SARAH - FAITH, PATIENCE, AND GOD'S PROMISE

## INTRODUCTION

The story of Sarah, the wife of Abraham, is a powerful testament to the importance of faith, patience, and trust in God's timing. As one of the matriarchs of the Bible, Sarah's journey is marked by both triumphs and struggles, particularly in relation to her desire to bear a child. Her story, found in the book of Genesis, offers valuable lessons for believers today, especially in a world that often prioritizes immediate gratification over patient endurance.

In this chapter, we will explore Sarah's life, focusing on her anxiety and impatience in the face of God's promise of a child. We will examine the consequences of her decision to take matters into her own hands, which led to the birth of Ishmael and the disrespect she faced from Hagar. Through Sarah's story, we will learn the importance of waiting patiently on the Lord and trusting in His perfect timing.

The chapter will be structured as follows:

1. The Promise of a Child
2. Sarah's Impatience and the Birth of Ishmael
3. The Consequences of Taking Matters into Our Own Hands
4. God's Faithfulness and the Birth of Isaac

5. The Importance of Patience in the Christian Life
6. Embracing God's Timing and Purpose
7. Lessons from Sarah's Life for Believers Today

Following these sections, we will provide a series of heartfelt prayers inspired by Sarah's story. These prayers will be divided into four categories:

a. Prayers for mercy for mistakes made due to impatience

b. Prayers against anxiety

c. Prayers to wait patiently on the Lord

d. Prayers to receive your Isaac: Oh Lord, cause me to laugh

Each prayer section will include ten prayer points, providing a total of 40 targeted prayers. These prayers will serve as a source of encouragement, comfort, and strength for those who, like Sarah, find themselves struggling with impatience, anxiety, and the temptation to take matters into their own hands.

Through this chapter, may we be reminded of the importance of faith, patience, and trust in God's timing. May we find hope in the knowledge that, no matter our past mistakes or present struggles, God's promises remain true, and His plans for our lives are always good.

**The Promise of a Child**

Sarah's story begins with a promise from God to her husband, Abraham. In Genesis 12:2-3, God declares to Abraham, "I will make you into a great nation, and I will bless you; I will make your name great, and you will be a blessing. I will bless those who bless you, and whoever curses you I will curse; and all peoples on earth will be blessed through you." This promise, which includes the assurance of numerous descendants, is later reiterated in Genesis 15:4-5, where God tells Abraham that his own son will be his heir and that his offspring will be as numerous as the stars in the sky.

At the time of these promises, both Abraham and Sarah are

advanced in age, and Sarah is barren. The idea of bearing a child seems impossible from a human perspective, but God's promise remains steadfast. As the years pass without the fulfillment of the promise, Sarah's faith is tested, and her impatience grows.

## Sarah's Impatience and the Birth of Ishmael

In Genesis 16, we see Sarah's impatience reach a critical point. After years of waiting for God's promise to be fulfilled, Sarah takes matters into her own hands. She gives her Egyptian servant, Hagar, to Abraham as a second wife, believing that perhaps she can build a family through her. Abraham agrees, and Hagar conceives a child.

However, this decision leads to tension and discord within the household. When Hagar realizes she is pregnant, she begins to despise Sarah. In response, Sarah mistreats Hagar, ultimately causing her to flee into the wilderness. This series of events highlights the consequences of attempting to force God's hand and the importance of waiting on His timing.

## The Consequences of Taking Matters into Our Own Hands

Sarah's decision to give Hagar to Abraham has far-reaching consequences. Hagar's son, Ishmael, becomes a source of tension and conflict within the family. In Genesis 21, after Isaac is born, Sarah sees Ishmael mocking and demands that Abraham send Hagar and Ishmael away. This painful decision is a direct result of Sarah's earlier impatience and lack of faith in God's timing.

The story of Ishmael and Isaac serves as a powerful reminder that our attempts to control or manipulate circumstances can lead to complications and heartache. When we step outside of God's will and try to force our own solutions, we often create additional problems and hinder the fulfillment of God's best plans for our lives.

## God's Faithfulness and the Birth of Isaac

Despite Sarah's impatience and the consequences of her actions,

God remains faithful to His promise. In Genesis 18, the Lord appears to Abraham and reaffirms that Sarah will bear a son within the next year. Sarah, overhearing this conversation, laughs to herself in disbelief, considering her advanced age. However, the Lord responds, "Is anything too hard for the Lord? I will return to you at the appointed time next year, and Sarah will have a son" (Genesis 18:14).

True to His word, God enables Sarah to conceive, and she gives birth to Isaac, whose name means "laughter" or "he laughs." The birth of Isaac is a testament to God's faithfulness and His ability to fulfill His promises, even when circumstances seem impossible. It also serves as a reminder that God's timing is always perfect, and His plans are not hindered by human limitations or doubts.

**The Importance of Patience in the Christian Life**

Sarah's story highlights the crucial role of patience in the life of a believer. In a world that often demands instant gratification and quick solutions, it can be challenging to wait upon the Lord and trust in His timing. However, as we see in Sarah's life, attempting to rush or manipulate God's plans can lead to painful consequences and hinder the fulfillment of His best for us.

The Bible repeatedly emphasizes the importance of patience and endurance in the Christian walk. Hebrews 6:12 encourages us to imitate those who through faith and patience inherit the promises of God. James 1:4 reminds us to let patience have its perfect work, that we may be perfect and complete, lacking nothing. These passages underscore the truth that spiritual growth and the fulfillment of God's promises often require a steadfast commitment to waiting on His timing.

**Embracing God's Timing and Purpose**

One of the key lessons from Sarah's life is the importance of embracing God's timing and purpose for our lives. While the waiting process can be challenging, it is often during these times that God is preparing us and aligning circumstances for the fulfillment of His plans. Like a seed that must go through a period of gestation before it bears fruit, our dreams and desires often require a season of waiting and growth before they come to fruition.

Sarah's story also reminds us that God's plans are often different from our own. The destiny of Isaac, the child of promise, was far greater than Sarah could have imagined. His birth set in motion the fulfillment of God's covenant with Abraham and paved the way for the coming of Jesus Christ. When we trust in God's timing and surrender our plans to Him, we open ourselves up to the incredible purposes He has for our lives, purposes that may exceed our wildest dreams.

**Lessons from Sarah's Life for Believers Today**

Sarah's story offers several valuable lessons for believers today:

1. Trust in God's promises: Despite the challenges and delays we may face, we can trust that God's promises are true and that He is faithful to fulfill them in His perfect timing.

2. Resist the temptation to rush God's plans: When we face periods of waiting or uncertainty, it can be tempting to take matters into our own hands. However, Sarah's story reminds us that attempting to force or manipulate circumstances can lead to painful consequences and hinder the fulfillment of God's best for us.

3. Embrace patience as a spiritual discipline: Waiting on God's timing requires a commitment to patience and endurance. As we cultivate these qualities in our lives, we open ourselves up to deeper spiritual growth and the development of a more intimate relationship with Christ.

4. Surrender your plans to God: Like Sarah, we may have our own ideas about how our lives should unfold.

However, when we surrender our plans to God and trust in His wisdom, we position ourselves to receive the incredible blessings and purposes He has for us.

5. Find hope in God's faithfulness: Sarah's story is a testament to God's faithfulness, even in the face of human doubts and limitations. As we navigate the challenges and uncertainties of life, we can find hope in the knowledge that our God is always true to His word and that His love for us never fails.

As we reflect on the life of Sarah, may we be encouraged to embrace faith, patience, and trust in God's timing. May her story inspire us to let go of our own agendas and surrender our lives to the perfect plans and purposes of our loving Heavenly Father.

**Prayers for Mercy for Mistakes Made Due to Impatience**

1. Heavenly Father, I come before You today, acknowledging the times when I have allowed impatience to lead me into making mistakes. Like Sarah, I have struggled to wait on Your timing and have taken matters into my own hands. I ask for Your mercy and forgiveness for these moments of weakness. Please help me to learn from my errors and to trust more fully in Your perfect plan. In Jesus' name, Amen.

2. Gracious God, I confess that I have often tried to rush Your plans and have acted out of impatience rather than faith. I know that my attempts to control situations have led to complications and have hindered the fulfillment of Your best for my life. I humbly ask for Your mercy and grace to cover my mistakes. Help me to surrender my timeline to You and to trust in Your wisdom. In Jesus' name, Amen.

3. Loving Father, I recognize that my impatience has sometimes caused hurt and discord in my relationships, just as Sarah's actions led to tension and generational discord. I ask for Your mercy and healing

for any pain I have caused others due to my lack of patience. Please help me to seek reconciliation where needed and to extend the same grace and forgiveness that You have shown me. In Jesus' name, Amen.

4. Merciful God, I know that my impatience often stems from a lack of trust in Your goodness and faithfulness. Forgive me for the times I have doubted Your promises and have tried to take control of my own life. I ask for Your mercy to cover my unbelief and for Your Holy Spirit to renew a steadfast spirit within me. Teach me to wait patiently on You, knowing that Your ways are always better than my own. In Jesus' name, Amen.

5. Compassionate Father, I come before You, acknowledging the times when my impatience has led me to make impulsive decisions that have had negative consequences. I ask for Your mercy and forgiveness for these mistakes. Please help me to learn to pause and seek Your guidance before acting, trusting that Your timing and wisdom are perfect. In Jesus' name, Amen.

6. Gracious God, I confess that I have sometimes allowed my impatience to lead me into sin, such as anger, frustration, or trying to control others. I ask for Your mercy and forgiveness for these moments of weakness. Please help me to cultivate the fruit of the Spirit in my life, especially patience, gentleness, and self-control. May my life reflect Your character and bring glory to Your name. In Jesus' name, Amen.

7. Loving Father, I recognize that my impatience often stems from a desire to have my own way or to see my own plans come to fruition. Forgive me for the times I have placed my own desires above Yours and have failed to trust in Your perfect will. I ask for Your mercy and grace to transform my heart and mind, aligning my desires with Yours and teaching me to find joy in

the journey of faith. In Jesus' name, Amen.

8. Merciful God, I know that my impatience can sometimes lead me to compare my life and circumstances to others, causing discontentment and frustration. Forgive me for the times I have failed to trust in Your unique plan and timing for my life. I ask for Your mercy and peace to fill my heart, helping me to find contentment and gratitude in every season. In Jesus' name, Amen.

9. Compassionate Father, I come before You, acknowledging the times when my impatience has caused me to speak or act in haste, leading to regret and the need for forgiveness. I ask for Your mercy and grace to cover these moments and for Your wisdom to guide my words and actions in the future. Help me to be quick to listen, slow to speak, and slow to become angry, reflecting Your love and patience to those around me. In Jesus' name, Amen.

10. Gracious God, I recognize that my journey of faith is a lifelong process of growth and transformation. I ask for Your mercy and patience with me as I continue to learn and mature in my walk with You. Help me to extend that same mercy and grace to myself and others, trusting that You are faithful to complete the good work You have begun in me. May I rest in Your love and timing, knowing that Your plans for me are always good. In Jesus' name, Amen.

## Prayers Against Anxiety

1. Heavenly Father, I come before You today, laying my anxieties and fears at Your feet. Like Sarah, I have struggled with worry and doubt, especially when it comes to waiting on Your promises. I pray that You would fill me with Your perfect peace, reminding me that You are in control and that Your plans for me are

good. Help me to cast all my cares upon You, knowing that You care for me. In Jesus' name, Amen.

2. Gracious God, I confess that anxiety has often robbed me of the joy and contentment You desire for me. I pray that You would help me to trust in Your timing and providence, even when circumstances seem uncertain or overwhelming. Teach me to fix my eyes on You, rather than on my worries, and to find rest in Your unchanging love and faithfulness. In Jesus' name, Amen.

3. Loving Father, I recognize that my anxiety often stems from a desire to control my own life and future. I pray that You would help me to surrender my plans and expectations to You, trusting that Your ways are higher than my own. Give me the faith to believe that You are working all things together for my good and Your glory, even when I cannot see the full picture. In Jesus' name, Amen.

4. Merciful God, I know that anxiety can be a heavy burden to bear, weighing down my heart and mind. I pray that You would lift this burden from me and replace it with Your joy and peace. Help me to meditate on Your promises and to find strength in Your presence, knowing that You are with me always. In Jesus' name, Amen.

5. Compassionate Father, I come before You, acknowledging the times when anxiety has caused me to doubt Your goodness and faithfulness. I pray that You would renew my mind and help me to take every thought captive to the obedience of Christ. Teach me to dwell on what is true, noble, right, pure, lovely, admirable, excellent, and praiseworthy, finding peace in the truth of Your Word. In Jesus' name, Amen.

6. Gracious God, I pray that You would help me to

cultivate a spirit of gratitude and contentment, even in the midst of my anxieties. Remind me of the countless blessings You have already bestowed upon me and the ways in which You have been faithful in the past. Help me to focus on Your goodness and mercy, trusting that You will continue to provide for all my needs. In Jesus' name, Amen.

7. Loving Father, I recognize that anxiety can sometimes lead me to seek comfort and security in things other than You. I pray that You would help me to find my ultimate peace and satisfaction in You alone. Teach me to rely on Your strength and wisdom, rather than on my own understanding or the temporary fixes of this world. In Jesus' name, Amen.

8. Merciful God, I know that anxiety can be a tool of the enemy, designed to distract me from Your purposes and steal my peace. I pray that You would protect my heart and mind from his attacks, and help me to stand firm in the truth of Your love and grace. Give me the courage to resist fear and worry, trusting in Your power to overcome every obstacle. In Jesus' name, Amen.

9. Compassionate Father, I come before You, lifting up all those who struggle with anxiety and fear. I pray that You would be their comfort and strength, reminding them of Your constant presence and unfailing love. Help them to cast their burdens upon You and to find rest in the shadow of Your wings. May they experience the peace that surpasses all understanding, guarding their hearts and minds in Christ Jesus. In Jesus' name, Amen.

10. Gracious God, I thank You for the assurance that nothing can separate me from Your love, not even my anxieties or fears. I pray that this truth would anchor

my soul and give me the confidence to face each day with faith and courage. Help me to trust in Your perfect plan and timing, knowing that You are working all things together for my good and Your glory. May my life be a testament to Your faithfulness and a source of hope and encouragement to others who struggle with anxiety. In Jesus' name, Amen.

## Prayers to Wait Patiently on the Lord

1. Heavenly Father, I come before You today, acknowledging my struggle to wait patiently on Your timing and plans. Like Sarah, I often find myself wanting to rush ahead or take control, rather than trusting in Your perfect will. I pray that You would help me to cultivate a heart of patience and faith, believing that Your ways are always best. Teach me to find joy and purpose in the waiting, knowing that You are using this time to shape me and prepare me for all that lies ahead. In Jesus' name, Amen.

2. Gracious God, I confess that waiting is not always easy, especially when I cannot see the end result or understand Your purposes. I pray that You would give me the strength and perseverance to wait upon You, even when the path seems long or uncertain. Help me to fix my eyes on Jesus, the author and perfecter of my faith, and to trust in Your faithfulness every step of the way. In Jesus' name, Amen.

3. Loving Father, I recognize that waiting on You requires a daily surrender of my own plans and desires. I pray that You would help me to lay down my own agenda and to embrace Yours, trusting that Your timing is always perfect. Teach me to be still and know that You are God, and to find my rest and security in Your unchanging love and grace. In Jesus' name, Amen.

4. Merciful God, I know that waiting can sometimes be a

painful and lonely process, as it was for Sarah. I pray that You would be my comfort and companion in the midst of the waiting, reminding me that I am never alone. Help me to lean into Your presence and to find strength in the fellowship of other believers who are also walking this path of faith and patience. In Jesus' name, Amen.

5. Compassionate Father, I come before You, asking for the grace to wait patiently on You, even when the world around me is rushing ahead. I pray that You would help me to resist the temptation to compare my journey with others or to seek instant gratification. Teach me to trust in Your unique plan and timing for my life, knowing that Your ways are always higher and better than my own. In Jesus' name, Amen.

6. Gracious God, I pray that You would use the times of waiting to deepen my faith and dependence on You. Help me to see these seasons as opportunities for growth and transformation, rather than as obstacles or delays. Teach me to pray without ceasing, to meditate on Your Word, and to seek Your face in every circumstance, knowing that You are working all things together for my good. In Jesus' name, Amen.

7. Loving Father, I recognize that waiting often requires a sacrifice of my own comfort and control. I pray that You would give me the willingness to lay down my own preferences and to embrace the challenges and opportunities that come with waiting on You. Help me to trust in Your provision and protection, knowing that You will supply all my needs according to Your riches in glory. In Jesus' name, Amen.

8. Merciful God, I know that waiting can sometimes feel like a battle, as I wrestle with doubts, fears, and impatience. I pray that You would arm me with the

truth of Your Word and the power of Your Spirit, enabling me to stand firm in faith and to resist the lies of the enemy. Help me to put on the full armor of God and to fight the good fight of faith, trusting in Your victory and strength. In Jesus' name, Amen.

9. Compassionate Father, I come before You, lifting up all those who are currently in a season of waiting and longing. I pray that You would be their hope and encouragement, reminding them of Your faithfulness and the beauty of Your plans. Help them to trust in Your timing and to find joy and purpose in the journey, knowing that You are always at work on their behalf. In Jesus' name, Amen.

10. Gracious God, I thank You for the gift of waiting, even though it is not always easy. I pray that You would use these times to mold me into the image of Christ and to prepare me for the incredible future You have in store. Help me to wait patiently and expectantly, knowing that You are a good Father who delights in giving good gifts to His children. May my life be a testament to the beauty and power of waiting on You, and may many come to know Your love and grace as a result. In Jesus' name, Amen.

## Prayers to Receive Your Isaac: Oh Lord, Cause Me to Laugh

1. Heavenly Father, I come before You today with a heart full of longing and desire, just as Sarah longed for a child of her own. I pray that You would hear the cry of my heart and grant me the desires that align with Your perfect will. Like Sarah, I believe that nothing is too hard for You, and I trust in Your power to bring forth life and laughter, even in the most impossible situations. Oh Lord, cause me to laugh with joy as You fulfill Your promises in my life. In Jesus' name, Amen.

2. Gracious God, I know that Your timing and plans are often different from my own, just as Sarah had to wait many years for the fulfillment of Your promise. I pray that You would give me the faith and patience to trust in Your divine timeline, knowing that Your ways are always best. Help me to find contentment and hope in the waiting, trusting that You are preparing me and aligning circumstances for the manifestation of my Isaac. Oh Lord, cause me to laugh with gratitude and amazement as I see Your hand at work in my life. In Jesus' name, Amen.

3. Loving Father, I recognize that the desires of my heart are not always in line with Your will, just as Sarah took matters into her own hands with Hagar. I pray that You would purify my motives and align my dreams with Your purposes, so that the Isaac I long for will bring glory to Your name. Help me to surrender my plans to You and to trust in Your wisdom and goodness, knowing that Your blessings are always better than anything I could scheme or imagine. Oh Lord, cause me to laugh with surrender and trust as I yield my life to You. In Jesus' name, Amen.

4. Merciful God, I know that the waiting process can sometimes be painful and discouraging, as Sarah experienced in her many years of barrenness. I pray that You would be my comfort and strength in the midst of the longing, reminding me of Your faithfulness and the beauty of Your plans. Help me to fix my eyes on You, rather than on my circumstances, and to find joy and purpose in Your presence. Oh Lord, cause me to laugh with hope and expectation, knowing that Your promises are always true. In Jesus' name, Amen.

5. Compassionate Father, I come before You, asking for the faith to believe in Your power to bring forth life

and laughter, even in the most barren and impossible situations. I pray that You would open my eyes to see the Isaacs that You have already placed in my life, and to celebrate the miracles that You are birthing, even now. Help me to trust in Your resurrection power and to hold fast to Your promises, knowing that You are able to do exceedingly abundantly above all that I could ask or think. Oh Lord, cause me to laugh with faith and wonder as I witness Your power at work. In Jesus' name, Amen.

6. Gracious God, I pray that You would use the story of Sarah to encourage and inspire me in my own journey of faith. Help me to remember that Your promises are not limited by human circumstances or limitations, and that Your power is made perfect in weakness. Teach me to hope against hope, to believe in Your goodness, and to trust in Your timing, knowing that You are always faithful. Oh Lord, cause me to laugh with anticipation and confidence, knowing that You are the God of the impossible. In Jesus' name, Amen.

7. Loving Father, I recognize that the birth of Isaac was not just a personal blessing for Sarah, but a part of Your greater plan of redemption for the world. I pray that You would help me to see my own desires and dreams in the context of Your kingdom purposes, and to trust that You are weaving my story into Your grand tapestry of grace. Help me to surrender my Isaacs to You, knowing that Your plans are always better and more beautiful than my own. Oh Lord, cause me to laugh with gratitude and awe as I see Your redemptive purposes unfold in my life. In Jesus' name, Amen.

8. Merciful God, I know that the enemy often tries to rob me of my laughter and joy, just as Sarah was tempted to doubt and despair in her waiting. I pray that You would protect my heart and mind from his lies and

discouragement, and help me to stand firm in the truth of Your love and faithfulness. Teach me to fight the good fight of faith, to put on the garment of praise, and to rejoice in You always, knowing that Your joy is my strength. Oh Lord, cause me to laugh with victory and triumph, knowing that You have already won the battle. In Jesus' name, Amen.

9. Compassionate Father, I come before You, lifting up all those who are waiting and longing for their own Isaacs, whether it be a child, a spouse, a healing, or a dream fulfilled. I pray that You would be their comfort and hope in the midst of the waiting, reminding them of Your love and the beauty of Your plans. Help them to trust in Your timing and to find joy and purpose in the journey, knowing that You are always at work on their behalf. Oh Lord, cause them to laugh with expectation and faith, knowing that You are the God who brings life out of barrenness. In Jesus' name, Amen.

10. Gracious God, I thank You for the gift of laughter and the promise of joy, even in the midst of the waiting and longing. I pray that You would fill my heart with Your peace and presence, reminding me that true happiness is found in You alone. Help me to trust in Your goodness and to wait patiently for the fulfillment of Your promises, knowing that Your timing is always perfect. Oh Lord, cause me to laugh with abandon and delight, knowing that You are the source of all joy and the giver of every good and perfect gift. May my life be a testament to Your faithfulness and a beacon of hope to all those who are waiting and longing for their own Isaacs. In Jesus' name, Amen.

# CHAPTER 2: REBECCA - DIVINE CONNECTIONS AND ANSWERED PRAYERS

## INTRODUCTION

The story of Rebecca, found in the book of Genesis, is a powerful testament to God's ability to orchestrate divine connections and answer the prayers of His people. As the wife of Isaac and the mother of Jacob and Esau, Rebecca plays a significant role in the unfolding of God's redemptive plan for humanity. Her journey is marked by moments of faith, obedience, and the miraculous intervention of God in the midst of barrenness and uncertainty.

In this chapter, we will explore the key events of Rebecca's life, beginning with the remarkable story of how God brought her into Isaac's life through the faithful prayers and actions of Abraham's servant. We will also delve into the challenges Rebecca faced in her own journey of faith, particularly her struggle with barrenness and the power of prayer in opening her womb.

As we study Rebecca's story, we will uncover valuable lessons about trusting in God's timing, seeking His guidance, and the importance of prayer in every season of life. We will see how God's hand was at work in Rebecca's life, even in the midst of difficult circumstances, and how He used her story to advance His purposes and bring glory to His name.

The chapter will be structured as follows:
1. Abraham's Charge to His Servant
2. The Servant's Prayer and the Arrival of Rebecca
3. Rebecca's Willingness and Faith
4. The Marriage of Isaac and Rebecca
5. Rebecca's Barrenness and Isaac's Prayer
6. The Birth of Jacob and Esau and the Fulfillment of God's Plan
7. Lessons from Rebecca's Life for Believers Today

Following these sections, this chapter provides a series of heartfelt prayers inspired by Rebecca's story. These prayers will be divided into two categories:

a. Prayers for marriage: destroy every delay and swiftly connect to your Isaac

b. Prayers for the fruit of the womb

Each prayer section will include twenty prayer points, providing a total of 40 targeted prayers. These prayers will serve as a source of encouragement, hope, and strength for those who, like Rebecca, are believing God for divine connections and breakthroughs in their lives.

Through this chapter, may we be inspired by Rebecca's faith and the power of prayer in the face of life's challenges. May we find hope in the knowledge that our God is a God of miracles, who is able to bring forth life and purpose, even in the most barren and impossible situations.

**Abraham's Charge to His Servant**

The story of Rebecca begins with Abraham, the great patriarch of the faith, who was now well advanced in years. With his wife Sarah having passed away and his son Isaac still unmarried, Abraham recognized the importance of securing a godly wife for his son, one who would help to carry on the covenant promises that God had made to him and his descendants.

In Genesis 24, we read of Abraham's charge to his oldest and most trusted servant, likely Eliezer of Damascus. Abraham instructed his servant to go back to his homeland, Mesopotamia, to find a wife for Isaac from among his own people. He made the servant swear an oath, stating, "I want you to swear by the Lord, the God of heaven and the God of earth, that you will not get a wife for my son from the daughters of the Canaanites, among whom I am living, but will go to my country and my own relatives and get a wife for my son Isaac" (Genesis 24:3-4).

Abraham's instructions were clear and specific, reflecting his deep faith in God's providence and his desire to ensure that Isaac's wife would share the same faith and values. He trusted that God would guide his servant and lead him to the right woman for his son, just as He had led Abraham throughout his own life.

**The Servant's Prayer and the Arrival of Rebecca**

Armed with his master's instructions and a strong faith in God, Abraham's servant set out on his journey to Mesopotamia. Upon arriving in the city of Nahor, he stopped at a well outside the city, knowing that this was a common place for women to gather and draw water. It was here that the servant prayed a specific and bold prayer, asking God to reveal the woman He had chosen to be Isaac's wife.

In Genesis 24:12-14, we read the servant's prayer: *"Lord, God of my master Abraham, make me successful today, and show kindness to my master Abraham. See, I am standing beside this spring, and the daughters of the townspeople are coming out to draw water. May it be that when I say to a young woman, 'Please let down your jar that I may have a drink,' and she says, 'Drink, and I'll water your camels too'—let her be the one you have chosen for your servant Isaac. By this I will know that you have shown kindness to my master."*

No sooner had the servant finished his prayer than Rebecca

appeared on the scene. The Bible describes her as "very beautiful" and "a virgin" (Genesis 24:16). When the servant asked her for a drink, she quickly offered him water and then went above and beyond, offering to draw water for his camels as well. This was a significant act of kindness and hospitality, as camels can drink up to 20-30 gallons of water at a time.

The servant, recognizing that his prayer had been answered, watched in amazement as Rebecca continued to draw water until all the camels had finished drinking. He then presented her with a gold nose ring and two gold bracelets, inquiring about her family and whether there was room in her father's house for him to spend the night.

Rebecca revealed that she was the granddaughter of Nahor, Abraham's brother, and that there was plenty of room for the servant and his camels. Upon hearing this, the servant bowed down and worshipped the Lord, saying, "Praise be to the Lord, the God of my master Abraham, who has not abandoned his kindness and faithfulness to my master. As for me, the Lord has led me on the journey to the house of my master's relatives" (Genesis 24:27).

**Rebecca's Willingness and Faith**

When Rebecca's brother Laban and her father Bethuel heard the servant's account of how God had led him to Rebecca, they acknowledged that this was indeed from the Lord. They gave their blessing for Rebecca to become Isaac's wife, stating, "Here is Rebecca; take her and go, and let her become the wife of your master's son, as the Lord has directed" (Genesis 24:51).

Rebecca's own faith and willingness to follow God's plan are evident in her response. When the servant requested to leave the next morning with Rebecca, her family asked her, "Will you go with this man?" (Genesis 24:58). Rebecca's reply was simple and profound: "I will go."

This decision would have required a great deal of faith and courage on Rebecca's part. She was leaving behind all that was familiar to her - her family, her home, and her culture - to travel to a foreign land and marry a man she had never met. Yet, she trusted in the God of Abraham and believed that this was His will for her life.

**The Marriage of Isaac and Rebecca**

When Rebecca arrived in Canaan, Isaac was in the field meditating. The Bible tells us that he "lifted up his eyes and looked, and there, the camels were coming" (Genesis 24:63). When Rebecca saw Isaac, she dismounted from her camel and asked the servant who he was. Upon learning that this was her future husband, she took a veil and covered herself, a sign of modesty and respect.

The servant then recounted to Isaac all that had happened and how God had led him to Rebecca. Isaac took Rebecca into the tent of his late mother Sarah, and she became his wife. The Bible tells us that "he loved her; and Isaac was comforted after his mother's death" (Genesis 24:67).

This beautiful story of God's providence and the coming together of Isaac and Rebecca in marriage is a testament to the faithfulness of God in guiding and providing for His children. It also highlights the importance of seeking God's will in matters of marriage and trusting in His perfect timing and plan.

**Rebecca's Barrenness and Isaac's Prayer**

Despite the joyous beginning of their marriage, Isaac and Rebecca soon faced a significant challenge: Rebecca was unable to conceive. The Bible tells us that "Isaac prayed to the Lord on behalf of his wife, because she was childless" (Genesis 25:21).

Isaac's prayer is a beautiful example of intercession and the importance of bringing our desires and struggles before the Lord. He didn't just pray once and give up; he pleaded with God on behalf of his wife, trusting in His power to open her womb and grant them children.

The Bible goes on to tell us that "the Lord answered his prayer, and his wife Rebecca became pregnant" (Genesis 25:21). This miraculous answer to prayer reminds us that nothing is too difficult for God and that He is able to bring forth life, even in the most barren of circumstances.

### The Birth of Jacob and Esau and the Fulfillment of God's Plan

Rebecca's pregnancy, however, was not without its challenges. The Bible tells us that "the babies jostled each other within her, and she said, 'Why is this happening to me?'" (Genesis 25:22). Troubled by this, Rebecca went to inquire of the Lord.

God's response to her was a prophetic word about the destiny of the two nations that would come from her sons: "Two nations are in your womb, and two peoples from within you will be separated; one people will be stronger than the other, and the older will serve the younger" (Genesis 25:23).

This word from the Lord was a reminder that God's plans and purposes often defy human expectations and norms. It also foreshadowed the ongoing struggle and conflict that would characterize the relationship between Jacob and Esau and their descendants.

When Rebecca gave birth, the first to come out was Esau, who was red and hairy. The second was Jacob, who was born grasping Esau's heel. As they grew, the boys developed distinct personalities and preferences, with Esau becoming a skillful hunter and Jacob a quiet man who stayed at home.

The story of Jacob and Esau's birth and their subsequent lives is a testament to God's sovereignty and His ability to work through even the most complex and difficult of family dynamics. It also highlights the importance of seeking God's wisdom and guidance in parenting and trusting in His perfect plan for our children's lives.

### Lessons from Rebecca's Life for Believers Today

Rebecca's story offers several valuable lessons for believers today:

1. Trust in God's providence: Just as God orchestrated the events that brought Rebecca into Isaac's life, we can trust that He is at work in our own lives, guiding and directing us according to His perfect plan.
2. Seek God's guidance in matters of marriage: Rebecca's story reminds us of the importance of seeking God's will in our relationships and trusting in His timing and provision for our marriages.
3. The power of prayer: Isaac's prayer on behalf of Rebecca's barrenness teaches us the importance of bringing our struggles and desires before the Lord and trusting in His power to bring forth life and fruit in our lives.
4. God's plans often defy human expectations: The prophetic word about Jacob and Esau's destinies reminds us that God's ways are often different from our own and that His purposes will ultimately prevail.
5. Seek God's wisdom in parenting: As parents, we can learn from Rebecca's story the importance of seeking God's guidance and wisdom in raising our children and trusting in His plan for their lives.

As we reflect on the life of Rebecca, may we be encouraged to trust in God's providence, seek His will in every area of our lives, and rely on the power of prayer to bring forth His purposes and plans. May her story inspire us to walk in faith and obedience, knowing that our God is faithful to guide and provide for us every step of the way.

## Prayers for Marriage: Destroy Every Delay and Swiftly Connect to Your Isaac

1. Heavenly Father, I come before You today, trusting in Your divine plan and purpose for my life, particularly in the area of marriage. Just as You orchestrated the events that brought Rebecca into Isaac's life, I pray

that You would guide and direct my steps towards the spouse You have chosen for me. Remove any obstacles or delays that may be hindering this connection, and bring us together in Your perfect timing. In Jesus' name, Amen.

2. Gracious God, I thank You for the gift of marriage and the beautiful example of love and commitment that Isaac and Rebecca's story provides. I ask that You would prepare my heart and the heart of my future spouse for the covenant of marriage. Help us to trust in Your timing and to wait patiently for Your perfect plan to unfold. Destroy any schemes of the enemy that would seek to delay or hinder our coming together. In Jesus' name, Amen.

3. Loving Father, I pray that You would give me the faith and courage to follow Your leading, even when the path ahead is uncertain. Just as Rebecca was willing to leave behind all that was familiar to her to follow God's plan, help me to trust in Your guidance and to step out in obedience to Your will. Destroy any fears or doubts that may be holding me back from embracing Your best for my life and my future marriage. In Jesus' name, Amen.

4. Sovereign Lord, I acknowledge that Your ways are often different from my own and that Your plans are always better than anything I could imagine. I surrender my desires and expectations for marriage to You, trusting that You know exactly what I need and who I need. Destroy any preconceived notions or human limitations that may be hindering me from receiving the spouse You have chosen for me. Help me to trust in Your divine orchestration and to wait expectantly for Your perfect timing. In Jesus' name, Amen.

5. Merciful God, I confess any areas of impatience, frustration, or bitterness in my heart regarding the delay in my marital connection. I pray that You would forgive me for any moments of unbelief or for trying to take matters into my own hands. Destroy any root of negativity or hopelessness that may be hindering my faith, and help me to trust in Your unfailing love and faithfulness. Renew my joy and peace as I wait upon You. In Jesus' name, Amen.

6. Gracious Father, I pray that You would be preparing and shaping my future spouse, even now. Wherever they may be, I ask that You would be drawing them closer to Yourself, molding their character, and aligning their heart with Yours. Destroy any ungodly relationships or influences that may be hindering their spiritual growth or their readiness for marriage. Bring us together in Your perfect timing and way. In Jesus' name, Amen.

7. Loving God, I thank You for the example of Abraham's servant, who sought Your guidance and direction in finding a spouse for Isaac. I pray that You would surround me with wise and godly counselors who can offer guidance and support as I navigate this season of waiting and preparation. Destroy any voices of doubt, criticism, or discouragement that may be speaking into my life, and help me to tune my ear to Your still, small voice. In Jesus' name, Amen.

8. Sovereign Lord, I pray that You would give me the wisdom and discernment to recognize the spouse that You have chosen for me. Just as Abraham's servant prayed for a specific sign to confirm Your will, I ask that You would make Your plans and purposes clear to me. Destroy any confusion, uncertainty, or mixed signals, and give me the faith and courage to trust in Your divine leading. In Jesus' name, Amen.

9. Merciful God, I lift up any past hurts, disappointments, or failed relationships that may be hindering my ability to trust in Your plan for my future marriage. I pray that You would bring healing and restoration to my heart, and that You would destroy any walls or barriers that I may have put up as a result of pain or fear. Help me to open my heart to the love and blessings that You have in store for me. In Jesus' name, Amen.

10. Gracious Father, I thank You for the hope and assurance that Your plans for me are good and that Your love for me is unfailing. I trust in Your ability to bring beauty from ashes and to redeem even the most broken of circumstances. Destroy any lies of the enemy that would seek to rob me of my joy and confidence in You. Help me to fix my eyes on You and to wait with eager anticipation for the spouse and the future You have prepared for me. In Jesus' name, Amen.

## Warfare Prayers for Marriage

1. I declare that every power or principality that is standing against my marital destiny will be frustrated and brought to confusion, in the name of Jesus. I break their influence over my life and relationships, and I declare that they will not succeed in hindering God's plan for my marriage. Amen.

2. Heavenly Father, I ask that You would develop in me the maturity, wisdom, and character that I need to be a godly and effective spouse. Help me to grow in every area of my life, so that I will be fully prepared for the responsibilities and challenges of marriage. In Jesus' name, Amen.

3. I break every satanic embargo and restriction that has been placed upon my marital life. I declare that every hindrance and obstacle to my marriage is now

lifted, and that I am free to move forward into the relationship that God has ordained for me. In Jesus' name, Amen.

4. I command every weapon that has been formed against my marital destiny to be rendered ineffective and powerless. I declare that no scheme of the enemy will succeed in keeping me from the spouse that God has chosen for me, and that every attack against my marriage will fall to the ground. In Jesus' name, Amen.

5. I loose myself from every form of marital delay, frustration, and stagnation that the enemy has planned for me. I declare that I am free to enter into the marriage that God has designed for me, and that no power of darkness will be able to hold me back. In Jesus' name, Amen.

6. I reject every satanic offer or counterfeit that is seeking to lure me away from God's perfect will for my marital life. I declare that I will not be deceived or enticed by any relationship that is not ordained by God, and that I will have the discernment to recognize and avoid every trap of the enemy. In Jesus' name, Amen.

7. I plead the blood of Jesus over my marital destiny and ask that it would speak my God-ordained spouse into existence. I declare that the power of the blood will break every curse, cancel every evil decree, and release the fulfillment of every promise that God has made concerning my marriage. In Jesus' name, Amen.

8. Heavenly Father, I ask that You would blot out completely every mistake and transgression of my ancestors that may be hindering my marital destiny. I thank You that the blood of Jesus cleanses me from every generational iniquity and breaks every curse that may have been passed down to me. In Jesus' name, Amen.

9. I declare that every enemy of God's plan for my marital life will be put to shame and brought to defeat. I ask that You would vindicate me from every false accusation and lie of the enemy, and that You would cause my marital destiny to shine forth as a testimony of Your goodness and faithfulness. In Jesus' name, Amen.

10. I ask that You would guide me to the partner that You have chosen for me - someone who will be compatible with the purpose and destiny that You have ordained for my life. I trust in Your wisdom and sovereignty to bring me together with a spouse who will help me to fulfill Your calling and bring glory to Your name. In Jesus' name, Amen.

11. Heavenly Father, I ask that You would bless me with a spouse who is after Your own heart - someone who will love me unconditionally, support me in my walk with You, and partner with me in building a godly marriage and family. I trust in Your perfect provision and timing, and I thank You in advance for the gift of a joyful and fulfilling marriage. In Jesus' mighty name, Amen.

## Prayers for the Fruit of the Womb

1. Heavenly Father, I come before You today, acknowledging that every good and perfect gift comes from You, including the gift of children. I pray that You would open my womb and bless me with the fruit of the womb, just as You answered Isaac's prayer and enabled Rebecca to conceive. I trust in Your power to bring forth life, even in the most barren of circumstances. In Jesus' name, Amen.

2. Gracious God, I thank You for the beautiful example of faith and perseverance that Isaac and Rebecca's story provides. I pray that You would give me the same spirit

of faith to believe in Your promises and to trust in Your timing for my conception and pregnancy. Help me to lean on You for strength and courage, even in the face of discouragement or delay. In Jesus' name, Amen.

3. Loving Father, I pray that You would remove any physical, emotional, or spiritual barriers that may be hindering my ability to conceive. I ask that You would bring healing and wholeness to my body, and that You would create a nurturing environment in my womb for a child to grow and thrive. I trust in Your power to do exceedingly abundantly above all that I could ask or think. In Jesus' name, Amen.

4. Sovereign Lord, I acknowledge that every life is a gift from You and that children are a heritage from the Lord. I pray that You would bless my husband and me with the gift of a child, and that You would use our family to bring glory and honor to Your name. Help us to trust in Your perfect plan and timing for our lives, and to surrender our desires and dreams into Your loving hands. In Jesus' name, Amen.

5. Merciful God, I confess any areas of fear, doubt, or unbelief that may be hindering my faith for conception. I pray that You would forgive me for any moments of questioning Your goodness or doubting Your ability to bring forth life in my womb. Help me to stand firm on Your promises and to trust in Your unfailing love and faithfulness. Renew my hope and strengthen my faith as I wait upon You. In Jesus' name, Amen.

6. Gracious Father, I pray that You would be preparing my body, my mind, and my heart for the journey of pregnancy and motherhood. I ask that You would fill me with Your peace and joy, and that You would give me the strength and wisdom to embrace the changes

and challenges that lie ahead. Help me to trust in Your sustaining grace and to rely on Your guidance every step of the way. In Jesus' name, Amen.

7. Loving God, I thank You for the godly examples of motherhood that You have placed in my life. I pray that You would surround me with wise and compassionate women who can offer encouragement, support, and prayer as I believe You for the blessing of children. Help me to glean from their wisdom and to find comfort in their friendship. In Jesus' name, Amen.

8. Sovereign Lord, I pray that You would give my husband and me the unity and agreement we need as we trust You for the gift of a child. I ask that You would strengthen our marriage and deepen our love for one another, and that You would use this season of waiting to draw us closer to each other and to You. Help us to be a support and encouragement to one another as we hold fast to Your promises. In Jesus' name, Amen.

9. Merciful God, I lift up any feelings of inadequacy, insecurity, or unworthiness that may be hindering my faith for motherhood. I pray that You would remind me of my true identity in Christ and that You would help me to see myself as You see me - beloved, chosen, and equipped for every good work that You have prepared for me. Help me to trust in Your sufficiency and to find my confidence in You alone. In Jesus' name, Amen.

10. Gracious Father, I thank You for the privilege and honor of partnering with You in the creation of new life. I pray that You would knit together in my womb the child that You have destined for our family, and that You would protect and nurture this precious life from the moment of conception. I dedicate my pregnancy and my child to You, trusting that Your

plans and purposes will be fulfilled in their life. May they grow to know and love You all the days of their life. In Jesus' name, Amen.

## Warfare Prayers for the Fruit of the Womb

1. Heavenly Father, I come before You today, believing in the miracle-working power of Your name. I declare that as I pray in the mighty name of Jesus, every barren situation in my life will be transformed, and I will experience the joy of childbearing. In Jesus' name, Amen.

2. Lord God, I stand against every handwriting, decree, or curse that has been issued against my ability to conceive and bear children. I command these negative pronouncements to be openly disgraced and rendered powerless by the fire of the Holy Spirit. In Jesus' mighty name, Amen.

3. I take authority over every demonic spirit and principality that has been assigned to hinder my fruitfulness and cause barrenness in my life. I command you to lose your hold and depart from me now, in the mighty name of Jesus Christ. Amen.

4. I declare that every power or force that has been blocking my womb and hindering my ability to conceive is now broken and defeated. I have won the victory through Christ Jesus, and no weapon formed against my fruitfulness shall prosper. In Jesus' mighty name, Amen.

5. I come against every power that has been prolonging my season of childlessness and causing delay in my conception. I declare that your influence is now broken, and your assignment against my life is terminated by the power of the Holy Spirit. In Jesus' name, Amen.

6. I tear down every altar that has been erected to hinder my ability to conceive and bear children. I command these altars to be scattered and destroyed by the thunder of God's power, and I declare that no sacrifice made against my fruitfulness shall prevail. In Jesus' name, Amen.

7. Gracious God, I ask that You would visit me with Your divine presence and power, just as You visited Rebecca and opened her womb. I trust in Your ability to break every cycle of barrenness and to bless me with the gift of children. In Jesus' mighty name, Amen.

8. I break every covenant of barrenness that may be operating in my father's family, my mother's family, or my spouse's family. I declare that these generational curses have no power over my life and that I am free to conceive and bear children according to God's perfect plan. In Jesus' name, Amen.

9. Your Word declares that children are a heritage from the Lord and that the fruit of the womb is a reward. I stand on this truth and refuse to accept barrenness as my portion. I believe that I will be surrounded by the blessing of children, according to Your promise. In Jesus' name, Amen.

10. I declare that by the power of Jesus Christ, which cannot be hindered, I will carry my pregnancies to full term and deliver healthy, thriving babies. No power of darkness will be able to interfere with the development or birth of my children. In Jesus' mighty name, Amen.

11. Miracle-working God, I ask that You would stretch forth Your hand of goodness and miraculously open my womb for conception. I believe that nothing is too hard for You and that You are able to bring forth life where there has been barrenness. In Jesus' name, Amen.

12. I bring every infection, disease, or spiritual attack that has been hindering my conception before the judgment seat of Christ. I command these afflictions to be consumed by the fire of God's presence and to be completely destroyed, in the mighty name of Jesus. Amen.

13. I command every witchcraft coven and satanic gathering that has been holding my womb captive to release their hold now, in the name of Jesus. I declare that their power is broken, and their schemes against my fruitfulness are forever destroyed. Amen.

14. Heavenly Father, I ask that You would breathe new life into any area of my body or my spouse's body that has been affected by barrenness. I believe that Your resurrection power is able to restore and regenerate every cell, tissue, and organ, making us fully fertile and able to conceive. In Jesus' name, Amen.

15. I release my reproductive system from any form of demonic control, manipulation, or oppression. I plead the blood of Jesus Christ over my ovaries, fallopian tubes, uterus, and every other organ involved in conception and childbearing. I declare that they are free to function according to God's perfect design. Amen.

16. I speak to my womb and command it to come alive with the breath of God. I declare that it is receptive to conception and that it will nurture and sustain every pregnancy to full term. I release the life-giving power of the Holy Spirit into my womb now, in Jesus' name. Amen.

17. Merciful Father, I repent of any generational sin that may have caused a curse of barrenness to be passed down through my family line. I ask for Your forgiveness and cleansing, and I believe that as You

heal my land, You will also heal my womb and make me fruitful. In Jesus' name, Amen.

18. I break every yoke of barrenness that has held me captive and prevented me from conceiving. I declare that I am now free from this prison of infertility, and I step into the liberty and fruitfulness that Christ has purchased for me on the cross. In Jesus' mighty name, Amen.

19. By the power of the blood of Jesus, I cancel every assignment of miscarriage that has been arrayed against my pregnancies. I declare that my babies will grow and thrive in my womb, and that I will carry them to full term and deliver them safely. In Jesus' name, Amen.

20. I come against every inherited bloodline of barrenness that may be operating in my spouse's family and affecting our ability to conceive. I command this curse to be broken now by the fire and thunder of God's power, in the mighty name of Jesus. Amen.

21. I declare that age is not a barrier to my fruitfulness, for nothing is impossible with God. I ask that You would stretch forth Your hand of power and rejuvenate my womb, causing it to be fully fertile and able to conceive and carry children. In Jesus' mighty name, Amen.

# CHAPTER 3: LEAH: THE MOST UNLOVED WIFE IN THE BIBLE

## INTRODUCTION

The story of Leah in the Bible is a poignant tale of a woman caught between the machinations of her deceitful father and the unloving heart of her husband. Born into a time when women had little to no rights, Leah's journey is a testament to the power of faith and the unfailing love of God in the face of seemingly insurmountable challenges.

In this chapter, we will delve into Leah's story, exploring the cultural context of her time, the circumstances that led to her marriage to Jacob, and the emotional turmoil she endured as the unloved wife. We will see how, despite her father's trickery and her husband's indifference, Leah's destiny was not thwarted, and how God used her to bring forth the lineage of the Messiah.

As we examine Leah's life, we will also draw parallels to the experiences of women today who find themselves in loveless marriages, facing challenges beyond their control, or struggling to find their place in the world. Through Leah's example, we will see how turning our hearts to God in praise and thanksgiving can be a powerful weapon in overcoming adversity and achieving our God-given destiny.

The chapter will be structured as follows:

1. The Cultural Context of Leah's Time

2. Leah's Marriage to Jacob: A Tale of Deception and Unlove
3. The Naming of Leah's Sons: A Reflection of Her Emotional Turmoil
4. Leah's Turning Point: From Seeking Love to Praising God
5. Leah's Legacy: The Mother of Judah and Levi
6. Lessons from Leah's Life for Women Today

Following these sections, this chapter provides a series of powerful prayers inspired by Leah's story. These prayers will be divided into three categories, each addressing a specific need or situation:

a. Prayers for women in a loveless marriage

b. Prayers to accomplish destiny in spite of your family background, circumstances beyond your control, and prevailing challenges

c. Prayers to receive favor and the highest honor from God

Each prayer section will include ten prayer points for both morning and night, providing a total of 60 targeted prayers. These prayers will serve as a resource for women who find themselves in situations similar to Leah's, offering hope, encouragement, and a reminder of God's unfailing love and power to transform even the most difficult circumstances.

Through this chapter, may we be inspired by Leah's resilience, moved by her faith, and encouraged to trust in God's plan for our lives, no matter the challenges we face. As we see how God honored Leah and used her life for His glory, may we be filled with hope and confidence that He can do the same for us.

**The Cultural Context of Leah's Time**

To fully understand Leah's story, it is essential to grasp the cultural context in which she lived. In the patriarchal society of ancient Israel, women had few rights and were largely under the authority of their fathers or husbands. Marriages were often arranged, and women were expected to fulfill their roles as wives and mothers without question.

In this context, Leah had little say in her own life. When her father, Laban, decided to deceive Jacob by substituting Leah for her younger sister Rachel on the wedding night, Leah had no choice but to comply. She was a pawn in her father's scheme, used to secure Jacob's labor for an additional seven years.

It is important to note that Jacob himself was no stranger to deception. He had previously deceived his own father, Isaac, and stolen the birthright from his brother, Esau. In a sense, Jacob was reaping what he had sown when Laban tricked him into marrying Leah.

Some Jewish texts suggest that Leah was originally intended to marry Esau. However, Esau's idolatrous ways and his choice of Hittite wives grieved his parents, Isaac and Rebekah, as recorded in Genesis 26:34-35: "When Esau was forty years old, he married Judith daughter of Beeri the Hittite, and also Basemath daughter of Elon the Hittite. They were a source of grief to Isaac and Rebekah." As a result, Leah may have been redirected to marry Jacob instead.

Regardless of the original plan, Leah found herself in a difficult situation, caught between a deceitful father and an unloving husband. Her story is a reflection of the challenges women faced in a society where they had little control over their own destinies.

## Leah's Marriage to Jacob: A Tale of Deception and Unlove

Leah's marriage to Jacob was marked by deception from the very beginning. Laban, Leah's father, had promised his younger daughter, Rachel, to Jacob in exchange for seven years of labor. However, on the wedding night, Laban secretly substituted Leah for Rachel, taking advantage of the evening's darkness and Jacob's intoxication.

When morning came, Jacob discovered the deception and confronted Laban. Laban justified his actions by claiming that it was not customary to marry off the younger daughter before the older. He then offered Rachel to Jacob in exchange for another seven years of labor, to which Jacob agreed.

From this point on, Leah found herself in a marriage characterized by unlove and competition with her sister. Jacob's heart belonged to Rachel, and he made no secret of his preference for her. Leah, on the other hand, was left to bear the pain of rejection and longing for her husband's affection.

The Bible records that "When the Lord saw that Leah was not loved, he enabled her to conceive, but Rachel remained childless" (Genesis 29:31). God's compassion for Leah's situation is evident in this verse, as He blessed her with fertility while Rachel initially struggled to conceive.

However, the blessing of children did not alleviate Leah's emotional turmoil. She named her sons in a way that reflected her deep yearning for Jacob's love and her hope that bearing him sons would change his heart towards her.

**The Naming of Leah's Sons: A Reflection of Her Emotional Turmoil**

Leah's emotional state can be clearly seen in the names she chose for her sons. Each name carries a significant meaning and reveals the depth of her pain and her longing for Jacob's love.

1. Reuben: Leah's firstborn son was named Reuben, which means "see, a son." Leah said, "It is because the Lord has seen my misery. Surely my husband will love me now" (Genesis 29:32). Leah hoped that providing Jacob with a son would earn his love and respect.

2. Simeon: Leah's second son was named Simeon, meaning "one who hears." She said, "Because the Lord heard that I am not loved, he gave me this one too" (Genesis 29:33). Leah acknowledged God's

compassion for her situation, but her words also reveal her continued pain at being unloved by Jacob.

3. Levi: Leah's third son was named Levi, which means "attached" or "joined." She said, "Now at last my husband will become attached to me, because I have borne him three sons" (Genesis 29:34). Leah's hope for Jacob's love persisted, and she believed that giving him a third son would finally win his affection.

4. Judah: Leah's fourth son marked a turning point in her life. She named him Judah, which means "praise," saying, "This time I will praise the Lord" (Genesis 29:35). Instead of focusing on her desire for Jacob's love, Leah chose to turn her heart to God in praise and thanksgiving.

Leah's journey through the naming of her sons reflects the emotional toll of being in an unloving marriage. Her persistent hope for Jacob's affection and her ultimate decision to find her worth in God's love is a powerful lesson for women facing similar circumstances today.

**Leah's Turning Point: From Seeking Love to Praising God**

The naming of Leah's fourth son, Judah, marked a significant shift in her perspective and approach to life. Instead of basing her worth and happiness on Jacob's love, she chose to focus on praising God.

This turning point in Leah's life teaches us a valuable lesson about the power of praise in the midst of difficult circumstances. When we shift our attention from our problems and pain to glorifying God, we open ourselves up to His transformative power and grace.

Leah's decision to praise God was not a magic solution that suddenly made her life perfect. She still had to navigate the challenges of being in a polygamous marriage and deal with the ongoing rivalry with her sister. However, her choice to find joy and purpose in her relationship with God gave her the strength and resilience to face these trials.

Psalm 34:1 says, "I will bless the Lord at all times; his praise shall continually be in my mouth." Leah's example encourages us to adopt this same attitude of constant praise, regardless of our circumstances. As we focus on God's goodness and faithfulness, we find hope, peace, and the courage to persevere.

**Leah's Legacy: The Mother of Judah and Levi**

Leah's legacy extends far beyond her personal story. Through her son Judah, she became an ancestor of Jesus Christ, the Messiah. Judah's descendants were promised the scepter of rulership, as recorded in Genesis 49:10, "The scepter will not depart from Judah, nor the ruler's staff from between his feet, until he to whom it belongs shall come and the obedience of the nations shall be his."

This prophecy finds its ultimate fulfillment in Jesus, the Lion of the tribe of Judah (Revelation 5:5). Leah's faithfulness and trust in God, despite her challenging circumstances, played a crucial role in the unfolding of God's plan of redemption for humanity.

Furthermore, Leah was the mother of Levi, whose descendants were chosen by God to serve as priests in Israel. The Levitical priesthood was responsible for maintaining the spiritual well-being of the nation and facilitating the people's relationship with God.

Leah's sons, Judah and Levi, represent two essential aspects of God's plan: the kingship and the priesthood. Through Leah, God brought forth the lineage of the Messiah and the spiritual leaders of His people. This incredible legacy stands as a testament to God's ability to use even the most challenging situations for His glory and purpose.

**Lessons from Leah's Life for Women Today**

Leah's story offers valuable lessons and encouragement for women today, particularly those who find themselves in difficult or unfulfilling relationships. Here are some key takeaways:

1. God sees and cares about your pain: Just as God saw Leah's misery and blessed her with children, He sees the struggles and heartaches of women today. He is not indifferent to your pain and desires to comfort and strengthen you.

2. Your worth is not defined by others' opinions: Leah's worth was not diminished by Jacob's lack of love for her. Similarly, your value as a person is not determined by your spouse, family, or anyone else. You are precious and loved by God, regardless of how others treat you.

3. Praise can transform your perspective: Leah's decision to praise God marked a turning point in her life. When we choose to praise God in the midst of our struggles, we invite His transformative power into our lives and gain a new perspective on our circumstances.

4. God can use your challenges for His glory: Leah's story is a testament to how God can use even the most difficult situations to accomplish His purposes. Trust that God is working in your life, even when things seem bleak, and believe that He can bring beauty from ashes.

5. Your legacy matters: Leah's faithfulness and trust in God had far-reaching impacts on the world through her descendants. Your choices and actions, even in the face of adversity, can leave a lasting legacy of faith and positively influence future generations.

6. Seeking God's Love Above All Else: One of the most profound lessons we can learn from Leah's story is the transformative power of seeking God's love above all else, especially in the face of a loveless marriage or difficult relationships. When Leah found herself in a marriage where she was unloved and overlooked, she

initially sought validation and love from her husband, Jacob. However, as her story progressed, we see a beautiful shift in her heart's focus.

Leah's journey teaches us that when we find ourselves in challenging relational circumstances, particularly in a loveless marriage, our primary response should be to turn our hearts toward God and seek His love above all else. This shift in focus not only brings healing and fulfillment to our own hearts but can also lead to unexpected blessings and honor from God.

The Bible reminds us in Matthew 6:33, "But seek first the kingdom of God and His righteousness, and all these things shall be added to you." This verse encapsulates the powerful truth that when we prioritize our relationship with God and align our lives with His purposes, He faithfully provides for our needs and desires in ways that often surpass our expectations.

For those finding themselves in situations similar to Leah's, here are practical ways to seek God's love and turn your heart toward Him:

a) Cultivate a lifestyle of praise: Like Leah, who named her fourth son Judah, meaning "praise," we can choose to focus on praising God regardless of our circumstances. Daily praise and worship shift our focus from our problems to God's greatness and faithfulness.

b) Engage in soul-winning: Sharing the love of God with others not only expands His kingdom but also fills our own hearts with His love and purpose. As we reach out to others with the gospel, we often find ourselves experiencing God's love in profound ways.

c) Participate in kingdom advancement activities: Actively involving yourself in activities that further God's kingdom, such as serving in your local church, participating in outreach programs, or supporting missions, can provide a sense of purpose and allow you to experience God's love through community and service.

d)   Develop a consistent prayer life: Regular, intimate conversation with God helps us to experience His love more deeply and to align our hearts with His will.

e)   Immerse yourself in Scripture: Spending time in God's Word allows His love and truth to permeate your heart and mind, bringing comfort, guidance, and transformation.

By focusing on winning the love of God through these practices, we position ourselves to experience His love in profound ways. God is love (1 John 4:8), and He remains faithful to those who earnestly seek Him. As we read in Jeremiah 29:13, "And you will seek Me and find Me, when you search for Me with all your heart."

When we make the conscious decision to shift our focus from seeking love and validation from others to seeking God's love wholeheartedly, we often find that He not only fills the void in our hearts but also decorates our lives with unexpected honor and blessings. Just as Leah, who was once unloved, became the mother of Judah (from whose line the Messiah would come) and Levi (from whom the priestly line would descend), God can take our seemingly hopeless situations and turn them into stories of divine favor and purpose.

Remember, in your pursuit of God's love, you are aligning yourself with the very essence of who He is. As you forget about the unlovingness of others and focus on winning the love of God through a lifestyle of daily praise, soul-winning, and kingdom advancement, you will find that God responds to your devotion in ways that far surpass human love and validation. May Leah's story inspire you to seek God's love above all else, trusting that as you do,

He will faithfully meet you, fill you with His love, and potentially use your life in ways you never imagined for His glory and the advancement of His kingdom.

As you navigate the challenges of life, draw strength and inspiration from Leah's story. Remember that you are not alone, and that God's love and purpose for your life remain steadfast, no matter the obstacles you face.

## Prayers for Women in a Loveless Marriage
*Morning Prayers*

1. Lord, I come before You today, acknowledging the pain and loneliness I feel in my marriage. Like Leah, I long for my husband's love and affection. I pray that You would soften his heart and help him to see me through Your eyes. Grant me the strength and grace to continue loving and serving him, even when it is difficult. In Jesus' name, Amen.

2. Heavenly Father, I thank You for seeing my misery and being attentive to my needs, just as You were to Leah. I pray that You would fill the void in my heart with Your unfailing love and help me to find my worth and satisfaction in You. Give me the courage to trust in Your plan for my life and my marriage. In Jesus' name, Amen.

3. God of all comfort, I ask that You would surround me with Your peace and presence today. Help me to let go of any bitterness or resentment I may be harboring towards my husband and give me the grace to extend forgiveness and compassion. May Your love flow through me and be a light in my marriage. In Jesus' name, Amen.

4. Mighty God, I pray that You would protect my heart and mind from the negative thoughts and emotions that can arise in a loveless marriage. Help me to take

every thought captive and to focus on what is true, noble, right, pure, lovely, and admirable. Give me the strength to persevere and to trust in Your goodness. In Jesus' name, Amen.

5. Loving Father, I pray that You would guide my words and actions today as I interact with my husband. Help me to speak with kindness, patience, and wisdom, even when it is difficult. May my conduct reflect Your love and grace, and may it be a testimony of Your transformative power in my life. In Jesus' name, Amen.

6. Merciful God, I lift up my husband to You today. I pray that You would touch his heart and draw him closer to You. Help him to understand the depth of Your love for him and to experience the joy and peace that comes from knowing You. Bring about a transformation in his life and in our marriage. In Jesus' name, Amen.

7. Sovereign Lord, I trust that You are in control of my life and my marriage. I pray that You would give me the faith and patience to wait upon You and to trust in Your timing. Help me to find contentment and joy in You, even in the midst of my challenges. May Your will be done in my life and in my marriage. In Jesus' name, Amen.

8. Gracious God, I thank You for the example of Leah and the lessons I can learn from her life. Help me to embrace the power of praise and to turn my heart towards You in gratitude, even when my circumstances are difficult. May my life be a testimony of Your faithfulness and love. In Jesus' name, Amen.

9. Compassionate Father, I pray that You would give me the strength and wisdom to be a godly wife, even in a loveless marriage. Help me to love my husband sacrificially, to respect him, and to support him. May my actions and attitudes bring honor to You and be a

reflection of Your character. In Jesus' name, Amen.

10. Almighty God, I thank You for Your unfailing love and constant presence in my life. I pray that You would fill me with Your hope and peace today, and help me to trust in Your plan for my life and my marriage. Give me the courage to face each day with faith and determination, knowing that You are with me always. In Jesus' name, Amen.

*Night Prayers*

1. Loving Father, as I come to the end of this day, I lay my burdens and heartaches at Your feet. I pray that You would comfort me and give me the peace that surpasses all understanding. Help me to rest in Your love and to trust in Your goodness, even in the midst of my struggles. In Jesus' name, Amen.

2. Gracious God, I thank You for sustaining me through another day in my loveless marriage. I pray that You would continue to give me the strength and grace I need to persevere and to love my husband, even when it is difficult. Help me to find my joy and satisfaction in You alone. In Jesus' name, Amen.

3. Merciful Lord, I confess any anger, bitterness, or unforgiveness that I may be holding onto in my heart. I pray that You would help me to release these negative emotions and to embrace Your love and compassion. Give me the grace to extend forgiveness to my husband and to trust in Your healing power. In Jesus' name, Amen.

4. Sovereign God, I pray that You would work in my marriage even as I sleep tonight. I ask that You would soften my husband's heart and draw him closer to You. Give him a desire to seek You and to love and cherish me as his wife. Bring about a transformation in our relationship and restore what has been broken. In

Jesus' name, Amen.

5. Faithful Father, I thank You for Your constant presence and unwavering love in my life. I pray that You would fill my dreams with Your peace and hope tonight. Help me to wake up tomorrow with a renewed sense of purpose and a determination to trust in Your plan for my life and my marriage. In Jesus' name, Amen.

6. Compassionate God, I lift up other women who are struggling in loveless marriages. I pray that You would comfort them and give them the strength and wisdom they need to persevere. Help them to find their hope and joy in You and to trust in Your plan for their lives. May they experience Your love and grace in a deep and powerful way. In Jesus' name, Amen.

7. Mighty Lord, I pray that You would protect my marriage from the attacks of the enemy. I ask that You would surround us with Your angels and shield us from any harm or manipulation. Help us to stand firm in our faith and to resist any temptation or deception that may come our way. In Jesus' name, Amen.

8. Gracious Father, I thank You for the gift of marriage and for the opportunity to love and serve my husband, even in difficult times. I pray that You would help me to be a blessing to him and to reflect Your love and grace in our relationship. May our marriage be a testimony of Your faithfulness and goodness. In Jesus' name, Amen.

9. Loving God, I pray that You would give me the patience and understanding I need to navigate the challenges of my loveless marriage. Help me to see my husband through Your eyes and to extend grace and kindness to him, even when it is difficult. May Your love be the foundation of our relationship. In Jesus' name, Amen.

10. Almighty Father, I entrust my marriage and my life into Your capable hands. I pray that You would work

all things together for my good and for Your glory, just as You did in Leah's life. Help me to trust in Your sovereignty and to rest in Your unfailing love. May Your will be done in my life and in my marriage. In Jesus' name, Amen.

## Prayers to Accomplish Destiny in Spite of Family Background, Circumstances Beyond Your Control, and Prevailing Challenges

*Morning Prayers*

1. Sovereign Lord, I thank You that my destiny is not determined by my family background or the circumstances I face. I pray that You would help me to trust in Your plan for my life and to embrace the unique purpose You have for me. Give me the faith and courage to pursue Your calling, no matter what obstacles I may encounter. In Jesus' name, Amen.

2. Gracious Father, I pray that You would give me the wisdom and discernment I need to navigate the challenges and circumstances beyond my control. Help me to make godly decisions and to seek Your guidance in every situation. May I trust in Your sovereignty and lean on Your understanding, rather than my own. In Jesus' name, Amen.

3. Mighty God, I ask that You would break any generational curses or negative patterns in my family that may hinder me from fulfilling my destiny. I pray that You would set me free from any bondage or limitation and help me to walk in the liberty and abundance that You have for me. May I be a trailblazer for future generations. In Jesus' name, Amen.

4. Faithful Lord, I pray that You would surround me with godly mentors, friends, and advisors who can encourage and support me as I pursue my destiny. Help me to be open to wise counsel and to be discerning

in my relationships. May I have the humility to learn from others and the courage to stand firm in my convictions. In Jesus' name, Amen.

5. Loving Father, I thank You for the unique gifts, talents, and abilities You have given me. I pray that You would help me to develop and use them for Your glory and to fulfill the purpose You have for my life. Give me the diligence and discipline to steward my gifts well and to pursue excellence in all that I do. In Jesus' name, Amen.

6. Merciful God, I pray that You would help me to overcome any fear, doubt, or insecurity that may hold me back from pursuing my destiny. Help me to find my confidence and identity in You and to trust in Your love and acceptance. May I have the courage to step out in faith and to take risks for Your kingdom. In Jesus' name, Amen.

7. Gracious Lord, I ask that You would open doors of opportunity for me to fulfill my destiny and to make a difference in the world. Help me to be sensitive to Your leading and to be ready to step through the doors You open. May I have the faith to trust in Your provision and timing, even when the path ahead is unclear. In Jesus' name, Amen.

8. Sovereign Father, I pray that You would help me to persevere through the challenges and setbacks I may face as I pursue my destiny. Give me the strength and resilience to keep going, even when things get tough. Help me to fix my eyes on You and to find my hope and joy in Your presence. May I finish the race You have set before me. In Jesus' name, Amen.

9. Loving God, I thank You for the example of Leah and other biblical heroes who accomplished their destiny in spite of difficult circumstances. I pray that You would help me to learn from their faith and

perseverance and to apply those lessons to my own life. May I trust in Your power to use all things for my good and Your glory. In Jesus' name, Amen.

10. Almighty Lord, I surrender my destiny and my future into Your hands. I pray that You would guide my steps and direct my path. Help me to seek Your will above all else and to trust in Your perfect plan for my life. May I fulfill the purpose You have for me and bring glory to Your name. In Jesus' name, Amen.

*Night Prayers*

1. Gracious Father, as I come to the end of this day, I thank You for Your faithfulness and guidance. I pray that You would continue to lead me and direct me as I pursue my destiny. Help me to trust in Your wisdom and to seek Your will in every decision I make. May I rest in Your love and grace tonight. In Jesus' name, Amen.

2. Sovereign God, I pray that You would give me the peace and assurance I need to face the challenges and uncertainties of tomorrow. Help me to remember that You are in control and that nothing can separate me from Your love. May I find my security and confidence in You alone. In Jesus' name, Amen.

3. Merciful Lord, I confess any areas of my life where I have allowed my circumstances or background to hold me back from pursuing my destiny. I pray that You would forgive me and help me to break free from any limiting beliefs or behaviors. May I embrace the truth of who I am in Christ and step into the fullness of Your plan for my life. In Jesus' name, Amen.

4. Loving Father, I thank You for the dreams and desires You have placed in my heart. I pray that You would help me to nurture and protect those dreams, even when faced with discouragement or opposition. Give me the

faith and perseverance to keep pursuing my destiny, no matter what obstacles I may encounter. In Jesus' name, Amen.

5. Mighty God, I ask that You would surround me with Your angels and protect me from any spiritual attacks or warfare that may come against me as I pursue my destiny. Help me to stand firm in my faith and to use the weapons of prayer and worship to overcome any darkness or opposition. May Your light and truth prevail in my life. In Jesus' name, Amen.

6. Gracious Lord, I pray that You would give me the wisdom and discernment I need to make godly choices and to avoid any pitfalls or distractions that may hinder my destiny. Help me to stay focused on Your plan and to prioritize my time and resources accordingly. May I be a good steward of all that You have entrusted to me. In Jesus' name, Amen.

7. Faithful God, I thank You for the unique story You are writing with my life. I pray that You would help me to embrace the journey and to trust in Your timing and provision. Give me the patience and perseverance to keep moving forward, even when the path ahead is uncertain. May I find joy and contentment in Your presence, no matter what my circumstances may be. In Jesus' name, Amen.

8. Loving Father, I lift up my family and loved ones to You tonight. I pray that You would bless them and help them to fulfill their own unique destinies. May we encourage and support one another in our journeys and be a source of strength and love for each other. Use our family to make a difference in the world and to bring glory to Your name. In Jesus' name, Amen.

9. Sovereign Lord, I pray that You would help me to be a light and a witness for You as I pursue my destiny. May

my life and my actions point others to Your love and truth. Give me the boldness and compassion to share my faith and to be a vessel of Your hope and healing to those around me. Use my destiny to impact lives for eternity. In Jesus' name, Amen.

10. Almighty God, I entrust my destiny and my future into Your capable hands. I pray that You would continue to guide and direct my steps, even as I sleep tonight. Help me to wake up tomorrow with a renewed sense of purpose and passion for the calling You have placed on my life. May I live each day with intention and devotion to You. In Jesus' name, Amen.

## Prayers to Receive Favor and the Highest Honor from God

*Morning Prayers*

1. Gracious Father, I come before You today with a humble and grateful heart. I thank You for Your unconditional love and acceptance, and I pray that You would grant me favor and honor in Your sight. Help me to live a life that is pleasing to You and to reflect Your character in all that I do. In Jesus' name, Amen.

2. Sovereign Lord, I acknowledge that all honor and glory belong to You alone. I pray that You would help me to seek Your approval above all else and to find my identity and worth in You. May I not be swayed by the opinions or expectations of others, but instead focus on fulfilling the unique purpose You have for me. In Jesus' name, Amen.

3. Loving God, I thank You for the gifts and talents You have given me. I pray that You would help me to use them for Your glory and to make a difference in the world. May I be a good steward of all that You have entrusted to me and use my resources and abilities to bless others and advance Your kingdom. In Jesus'

name, Amen.

4. Merciful Father, I confess any areas of pride or self-reliance in my life. I pray that You would help me to cultivate a spirit of humility and dependence on You. May I recognize that any favor or success I experience is a result of Your grace and not my own merit. Help me to give You all the honor and praise. In Jesus' name, Amen.

5. Mighty God, I pray that You would open doors of opportunity and favor for me in my life and work. Help me to be sensitive to Your leading and to step out in faith when You call me to take action. May I trust in Your provision and timing, even when the path ahead is unclear. Use me as a vessel of Your blessing and favor to others. In Jesus' name, Amen.

6. Gracious Lord, I ask that You would surround me with godly mentors and advisors who can offer wisdom and guidance as I seek to honor You with my life. Help me to be open to correction and instruction and to have a teachable spirit. May I learn from the examples of those who have gone before me and model integrity and faithfulness. In Jesus' name, Amen.

7. Loving Father, I pray that You would give me a heart of compassion and service towards others. Help me to use any favor or influence I have to make a positive difference in the lives of those around me. May I be a reflection of Your love and grace, and may my actions bring honor and glory to Your name. In Jesus' name, Amen.

8. Sovereign God, I thank You for the example of Leah and other biblical heroes who received favor and honor from You. I pray that You would help me to learn from their stories and to apply the lessons to my own life. May I trust in Your ability to exalt the humble

and to use even the most unlikely individuals for Your purposes. In Jesus' name, Amen.

9. Faithful Lord, I pray that You would help me to persevere in seeking Your favor and honor, even when faced with challenges or setbacks. Give me the strength and determination to keep pursuing righteousness and to trust in Your perfect plan for my life. May I find my joy and satisfaction in pleasing You above all else. In Jesus' name, Amen.

10. Almighty God, I surrender my desires for favor and honor into Your hands. I pray that You would align my heart with Yours and help me to seek first Your kingdom and righteousness. May I trust in Your ability to exalt and promote me in Your perfect timing and way. Use my life to bring glory and honor to Your name. In Jesus' name, Amen.

*Night Prayers*

1. Gracious Father, as I come to the end of this day, I thank You for Your faithfulness and goodness in my life. I pray that You would continue to grant me favor and honor as I seek to live for You. Help me to rest in Your love and grace tonight, knowing that my worth and value come from You alone. In Jesus' name, Amen.

2. Sovereign Lord, I pray that You would give me the wisdom and discernment I need to make godly choices and to avoid any pitfalls or temptations that may compromise my integrity or witness. Help me to be a person of character and conviction, even when it is difficult or unpopular. May I honor You in all that I do. In Jesus' name, Amen.

3. Loving God, I thank You for the blessings and favor You have already bestowed upon my life. I pray that You would help me to steward those blessings well and to use them to bless others in turn. May I be a conduit

of Your generosity and grace, and may my life be a testimony of Your goodness and provision. In Jesus' name, Amen.

4. Merciful Father, I confess any areas of my life where I have sought favor or honor from others instead of from You. I pray that You would forgive me and help me to realign my priorities and motivations. May I seek to please You above all else and find my identity and security in Your love and acceptance. In Jesus' name, Amen.

5. Mighty God, I ask that You would protect me from any attacks or schemes of the enemy that may seek to derail or discourage me as I pursue Your favor and honor. Help me to stand firm in my faith and to use the weapons of prayer and worship to overcome any obstacles or opposition. May Your will be done in my life. In Jesus' name, Amen.

6. Gracious Lord, I pray that You would surround me with a community of believers who can encourage and support me in my journey of faith. Help me to cultivate deep and authentic relationships with others who can hold me accountable and spur me on towards righteousness. May we honor and glorify You together. In Jesus' name, Amen.

7. Faithful God, I thank You for the unique story You are writing with my life. I pray that You would help me to trust in Your plan and timing, even when the path ahead is uncertain. Give me the faith and patience to keep seeking Your favor and honor, knowing that You are working all things together for my good and Your glory. In Jesus' name, Amen.

8. Loving Father, I lift up my family and loved ones to You tonight. I pray that You would bless them and help them to experience Your favor and honor in their

own lives. May we encourage and support one another in our journeys of faith and be a reflection of Your love and grace to the world around us. In Jesus' name, Amen.

9. Sovereign Lord, I pray that You would help me to be a light and a witness for You as I seek to live a life of honor and integrity. May my words and actions point others to Your goodness and truth, and may I be a vessel of Your love and compassion to those who are hurting or lost. Use me to impact lives for Your kingdom. In Jesus' name, Amen.

10. Almighty God, I entrust my life and my future into Your capable hands. I pray that You would continue to guide and direct my steps, even as I sleep tonight. Help me to wake up tomorrow with a renewed sense of purpose and passion for honoring You in all that I do. May Your favor and blessing be upon me, and may my life bring glory to Your name. In Jesus' name, Amen.

# CHAPTER 4: TAMAR – THE WRONGED WOMAN

## INTRODUCTION

The story of Tamar in Genesis 38 is a powerful example of how God can preserve a person's destiny amidst wickedness, injustice, and wasted years. Though Tamar faced repeated hardship and mistreatment from the family she married into, God had a plan to include her in the lineage of His promised Messiah.

In this chapter, we will explore Tamar's journey and the valuable lessons her story teaches us. We begin by summarizing the key events of Genesis 38, which introduce us to Tamar's plight and the wicked actions of her husbands and father-in-law. Next, we delve into the concept of levirate marriage, a custom that plays a central role in Tamar's story. By understanding this practice, we gain insight into the injustice Tamar faced and the way in which Judah failed to fulfill his duty to her.

The following section examines how God preserved Tamar's destiny despite the evil perpetrated against her. Through her bold assertion of power, Tamar secures her place in the lineage of Christ, even as Judah's Canaanite wife is cut off from this privilege. This demonstrates God's faithfulness to defend the destinies of those who trust in Him.

Tamar's story also serves as a warning against family wickedness and parental complicity in sin. We will explore the severe consequences that can result from such actions and the importance of raising children in righteousness. This section acts as a wake-up call to parents who enable or excuse their children's sinful behavior.

The chapter concludes with a series of powerful prayers inspired by Tamar's story. These prayers are divided into four categories, each addressing a specific need or situation:

1. Prayers for women married to wicked men and/or families
2. Prayers for deliverance from satanic/occultic families
3. Prayers for protection against wicked in-laws
4. Prayers to redeem your time and fulfill destiny after wasted years

Each prayer section begins with relevant scriptures for confession and meditation, followed by ten specific prayers. These prayers invite women facing similar challenges to cry out to God for deliverance, restoration, and purpose. They serve as a reminder that, like Tamar, we can trust God to redeem our painful pasts and bring us into our glorious destiny in Christ.

Through this chapter, may we be encouraged by Tamar's resilience, challenged by the warnings her story provides, and equipped with prayers to help us navigate the difficulties we face. As we see God's hand at work in Tamar's life, may we trust Him to do the same in ours.

## Summary of Genesis 38

Judah, one of Jacob's sons, marries a Canaanite woman and has three sons: Er, Onan, and Shelah. Judah arranges for his firstborn, Er, to marry a woman named Tamar. However, Er is wicked in the sight of the Lord, and the Lord puts him to death.

Following the custom of levirate marriage, Judah tells his second son, Onan, to marry Tamar and produce offspring for his deceased brother. Onan, knowing that the child would not be his, deliberately spills his semen on the ground to avoid providing offspring for his brother. This displeases the Lord, and He puts Onan to death as well.

Judah, fearing for his youngest son Shelah's life, sends Tamar back to her father's house, promising that Shelah will marry her when he grows up. However, Judah does not keep his promise.

After a long time, Judah's wife dies. Tamar, realizing that Shelah has grown up but has not been given to her in marriage, takes matters into her own hands. She disguises herself as a prostitute and sits by the road where Judah is going to shear his sheep. Judah, not recognizing her, sleeps with her and gives her his signet, cord, and staff as a pledge for payment.

When Judah sends his friend to give the prostitute a young goat as payment and retrieve his pledge, the woman is nowhere to be found. Three months later, Judah learns that Tamar is pregnant and orders her to be burned to death for prostitution. However, Tamar produces Judah's signet, cord, and staff, proving that he is the father of her child. Judah acknowledges his wrongdoing in not giving Shelah to her as promised.

Tamar gives birth to twin boys, Perez and Zerah. Perez becomes an ancestor of King David and, consequently, of Jesus Christ.

The story highlights themes of levirate marriage, the importance of producing heirs, and the unconventional means by which God's providence is sometimes worked out through human affairs.

**Tamar in a state of Limbo: Understanding Levirate marriage**

Levirate marriage was a custom in ancient Near Eastern societies, including ancient Israel. The term "levirate" comes from the Latin word "levir," meaning "husband's brother." According to this custom, if a married man died without producing a male heir, his brother was obligated to marry the widow and father a child with her. The firstborn son from this union would be considered the legal descendant of the deceased brother, ensuring the continuation of his family line and the preservation of his inheritance.

In the story of Tamar, we see that Judah's firstborn son, Er, died without producing an heir. Following the levirate marriage custom, Judah instructed his second son, Onan, to marry Tamar and produce offspring for his deceased brother. However, Onan, knowing that the child would not be considered his own, practiced coitus interruptus to avoid fulfilling this duty.

Onan's behavior demonstrated a callous disregard for Tamar's well-being and future security, as well as a refusal to honor his brother's memory and family obligations. He was content to use Tamar for his own sexual pleasure while denying her the opportunity to become a mother and secure her place in the family.

This selfish and deceitful act was viewed as wicked in the eyes of the Lord. The biblical text states that God's judgment fell upon Onan for this egregious violation of family duty and exploitation of Tamar, resulting in his death. This severe consequence underscores the seriousness with which God viewed the abuse of levirate marriage customs and the mistreatment of vulnerable widows.

Following the deaths of Er and Onan, Judah made a promise to Tamar that his third son, Shelah, would fulfill the levirate duty when he came of age. Under this arrangement, Judah sent Tamar back to her father's house to live as a widow. However, her situation was uniquely precarious. Unlike other widows who could remarry, Tamar was bound by the levirate law to Judah's family. This meant she was required to remain chaste, facing the threat of capital punishment (death) if caught in adultery, while waiting for a marriage that seemed increasingly unlikely to materialize.

As time passed, it became evident that Judah had no intention of fulfilling his promise. His reluctance likely stemmed from a superstitious fear that Shelah might suffer the same fate as his brothers if he married Tamar. By withholding Shelah, Judah not only denied Tamar the opportunity to fulfill her role in the levirate marriage and produce an heir for Er but also effectively consigned her to a state of limbo, wasting her childbearing years.

According to the levirate law, Judah had three legitimate options: he could give Tamar to Shelah as promised, perform the levirate duty himself if he had no son over ten years old, or formally release Tamar from her obligation, allowing her to marry outside the family. Instead, Judah chose none of these, leaving Tamar in a state of prolonged and unjust suspension, neither free to move on with her life nor able to fulfill her role within the family.

Judah's actions were a clear violation of the levirate marriage custom and a wrongdoing against Tamar. By not allowing her to marry Shelah, Judah left Tamar in a state of limbo - she was neither a virgin nor a wife, and her status as a childless widow limited her options in society. Tamar was denied the opportunity to secure her future through the birth of a son, which would have ensured her place in her deceased husband's family and provided for her in her old age.

Moreover, Judah's failure to fulfill his obligation to Tamar was a breach of trust and a disregard for her well-being. As a result, Tamar had to resort to unconventional means to seek justice and secure her future by deceiving Judah and conceiving a child with him. While her actions may seem morally questionable, they can be understood as a response to the injustice she faced and a way to assert her rights within the confines of her society's customs.

## God's Preservation of Tamar's Destiny Amidst Family Wickedness and Injustice

In the story of Tamar, we see a remarkable example of how God can preserve a person's destiny despite the wickedness, unfaithfulness, and selfishness of those around them. Tamar's journey was marked by hardship, injustice, and wasted years, yet God's divine plan for her life remained intact.

Tamar was originally married to Judah's firstborn son, Er, positioning her to be in the lineage of Jesus Christ. However, Er was wicked in the sight of the Lord, and God put him to death. This could have been the end of Tamar's destiny, but God had other plans.

Onan, Judah's second son, was then called upon to fulfill the levirate marriage duty and provide an heir for his deceased brother. However, Onan, too, was wicked and refused to fulfill his obligation, leading to his death at the hand of God. Once again, Tamar's destiny was threatened by the sinfulness of those around her.

Judah, who should have been Tamar's protector and provider, failed in his duty to give her in marriage to his third son, Shelah. Instead of releasing her to remarry or fulfilling the levirate marriage duty himself, Judah chose to waste Tamar's years by keeping her bound to his family without any intention of providing her with a husband. This left Tamar in a vulnerable position, with no husband, no children, no clear future, and years of her life wasted waiting for a promise that Judah never intended to keep.

However, God had not forgotten Tamar or her destiny. Through Tamar's bold assertion of power, she was able to conceive twins by Judah, ensuring that she would indeed be part of the lineage of Jesus Christ. God used Tamar's difficult circumstances, the wickedness of those around her, and the years she had lost to bring about His divine plan.

It is significant to note that Judah's wife, the mother of Er, Onan, and Shelah, who had been married to Judah for many years and bore him three sons, was ultimately cutoff from the lineage of Jesus. Initially, one might have expected the Messianic lineage to follow the pattern of Abraham (Sarah), Isaac (Rebecca), Jacob (Leah), and then Judah (Judah's wife). However, God's sovereign plan took an unexpected turn.

Instead of continuing through Shelah, the lineage of Jesus was redirected through the union of Judah and Tamar, which produced Perez. This dramatic shift in the family line underscores the unpredictable nature of God's redemptive work and His ability to bring about His purposes through unexpected means.

Strikingly, Judah's wife remains unnamed in the biblical narrative, her identity obscured as she was removed from Jesus' ancestral line. This omission serves as a sobering reminder of the severe consequences that can befall a family entrenched in wickedness, potentially leading to the loss of divine blessings and the forfeiture of a destined role in God's grand narrative.

This turn of events also highlights the critical role that parents, particularly mothers, play in shaping the moral character of their children. It stands as a cautionary tale for those who might be tempted to overlook or even encourage their children's misdeeds. The repercussions of such actions can extend far beyond immediate consequences, potentially altering the course of a family's legacy for generations to come.

The story of Tamar offers hope and encouragement to women who find themselves married into wicked families. It demonstrates that God is able to defend and preserve the destinies of those who trust in Him, even in the face of adversity and injustice. Tamar's faith and determination to secure her rightful place in God's plan can serve as an inspiration to women facing similar challenges.

The story of Tamar also offers hope and encouragement to women who find themselves in situations where their years are being wasted by the selfishness and unfaithfulness of others. It demonstrates that God is able to defend and preserve the destinies of those who trust in Him, even when it seems like time is being lost and promises are not being kept.

Ultimately, the story of Tamar highlights God's sovereignty and

His ability to work through even the most difficult, unjust, and seemingly hopeless circumstances to fulfill His purposes. It is a testament to the fact that no matter how much time seems to have been wasted, God is always in control and can bring about redemption and restoration for those who trust in Him.

**A Warning to Wicked Families and Complicit Parents**

The story of Tamar serves not only as an encouragement to those who face injustice but also as a stern warning to families who perpetuate wickedness and parents who are complicit in their children's sinful behavior.

Judah's family is a prime example of the consequences that can befall a household that engages in and enables wickedness. Judah's sons, Er and Onan, were both described as wicked in the eyes of the Lord, and their actions led to their untimely deaths. As a father, Judah had a responsibility to raise his sons in righteousness and correct their sinful behavior. However, he failed in this duty, and his complicity in their wickedness ultimately led to the loss of two of his sons.

Moreover, Judah himself acted wickedly by withholding his third son, Shelah, from Tamar and wasting her years. His selfish decision to prioritize his own fears and desires over his duty to Tamar and God's law showcases the depth of his own sinfulness.

This story should serve as a wake-up call to parents who turn a blind eye to their children's sinful behavior or, worse yet, actively encourage it. Mothers who enable or excuse their sons' wickedness and fathers who fail to discipline and guide their children in righteousness are setting their families up for disaster.

The Bible is clear that the sins of the parents can have lasting consequences on their children and future generations. Families that perpetuate cycles of wickedness and disobedience to God's laws risk incurring divine judgment and losing out on the blessings and destinies that God has in store for them.

Furthermore, the story of Tamar highlights the particular wickedness of mistreating and oppressing daughters-in-law. In many cultures, daughters-in-law are vulnerable members of the family, often at the mercy of their husband's parents and siblings. Wicked families may seek to exploit this vulnerability, as Judah did with Tamar, by withholding their rights, neglecting their well-being, and treating them as disposable.

However, God sees the plight of the oppressed and will not allow injustice to go unanswered. Families who mistreat their daughters-in-law risk incurring the wrath of God and facing the consequences of their actions.

In conclusion, the story of Tamar serves as a warning to families who engage in wickedness and parents who enable or encourage sinful behavior in their children. It is a reminder that God will not be mocked and that the consequences of sin can be severe and long-lasting. May all families take heed of this warning and strive to live in righteousness, justice, and obedience to God's laws.

**Lessons from Tamar's Story for Our Lives Today**

1. God's plans prevail despite human failings: Tamar's story demonstrates that God's purposes can be accomplished even through complex and morally ambiguous situations. Despite the failures of Er, Onan, and Judah, God's plan for the lineage of Christ was not thwarted. This reminds us that our mistakes or the wrongdoings of others cannot ultimately derail God's sovereign plans for our lives.

2. The importance of righteousness and justice: When Judah learns of Tamar's pregnancy, he initially condemns her without recognizing his own role in the situation. However, when confronted with the truth, he admits, "She is more righteous than I" (Genesis 38:26). This highlights the importance of self-reflection, honesty, and the pursuit of true

righteousness rather than mere adherence to social norms.

3. Cultural norms do not supersede God's justice: Tamar's story challenges the cultural norms of her time. She was willing to risk everything, including her life, to secure justice for herself and her future. This teaches us that there are times when we may need to challenge unjust systems or cultural expectations in order to align with God's higher standards of justice and righteousness.

4. God can redeem our past and use it for His glory: Despite the scandalous nature of Tamar's story, she is included in the genealogy of Jesus Christ (Matthew 1:3). This powerful inclusion reminds us that God can take even the most complicated and seemingly hopeless situations in our lives and use them for His glory and the fulfillment of His purposes.

5. Don't be docile about your destiny: Tamar's story powerfully illustrates that femininity does not equate to passivity, especially when it comes to matters of destiny. Her actions, though unconventional, demonstrate a fierce determination to secure her rightful place in God's plan. This teaches us several important lessons:

a) Don't allow anyone, including toxic family members or an unloving spouse, to rob you of your divine destiny. Your purpose is God-given and should be zealously guarded.

b) After seeking God's face in prayer, be prepared to take courageous steps of faith. If God is prompting you to make a bold move, do so without hesitation. Trust that He will provide and resettle you.

c) Recognize that no earthly relationship, including marriage, is worth sacrificing your God-ordained destiny. While we should strive to honor our commitments, we must also discern when a situation is hindering God's ultimate purpose for our lives.

d) If you find yourself in a situation where you've made a mistake in marriage or are dealing with a spouse who has turned from righteousness, remember that this does not signal the end of your destiny. God is able to rework circumstances to ensure His plans for you are fulfilled.

e) Develop a holy audacity in pursuing what God has promised you. Like Tamar, there may be times when you need to step out in faith and take action to align yourself with God's purposes.

f) Trust in God's ability to vindicate you and bring justice to your situation. Tamar's bold actions led to Judah declaring, "She is more righteous than I." Sometimes, our faith-filled actions can lead to unexpected reconciliation and restoration.

Tamar's story indeed exemplifies this lesson. She refused to passively accept the injustice done to her and took bold (albeit controversial) action to secure her rights and future. We can learn from her determination to pursue what was rightfully hers. This teaches us to be proactive in pursuing our God-given destiny, even when faced with obstacles or opposition. It reminds us that our identity and purpose in God supersede any earthly relationship or circumstance, and that with faith and courage, we can trust God to make a way where there seems to be no way. Embrace bold faith in pursuing your God-ordained destiny.

## Prayers for women married to wicked men and/or families

Scriptures for confession and meditation:

1. "The Lord is my light and my salvation; whom shall I fear? The Lord is the strength of my life; of whom shall I be afraid?" (Psalm 27:1)

2. "But the Lord is faithful, who will establish you and guard you from the evil one." (2 Thessalonians 3:3)

3. "No weapon formed against you shall prosper, and every tongue which rises against you in judgment you shall condemn. This is the heritage of the servants of the Lord, and their righteousness is from Me," says the Lord. (Isaiah 54:17)

4. "But You, O Lord, are a shield for me, my glory and the One who lifts up my head." (Psalm 3:3)

5. "The Lord will fight for you, and you shall hold your peace." (Exodus 14:14)

6. "And we know that all things work together for good to those who love God, to those who are the called according to His purpose." (Romans 8:28)

MORNING PRAYERS

1. Lord, give me the strength to endure the challenges of being married to a wicked spouse. Grant me your peace and protection, in Jesus' mighty name.

2. Father, I pray for the salvation of my husband and his family. Soften their hearts and draw them to your love and truth, in Jesus' mighty name.

3. God, help me to be a light in this dark situation. Give me wisdom and discernment to navigate the difficulties I face, in Jesus' mighty name.

4. Lord, shield me from the harmful influence of my husband's wickedness. Surround me with your angels and protect me from all evil, in Jesus' mighty name.

5. Heavenly Father, give me the courage to stand firm in my faith, even in the face of opposition from my spouse and his family, in Jesus' mighty name.

6. God, I pray for the transformation of my husband's heart. Let your Holy Spirit convict him of his sin and

lead him to repentance, in Jesus' mighty name.

7. Lord, help me to love my husband as Christ loves the church, even when it is difficult. Give me the grace to extend forgiveness and show compassion, in Jesus' mighty name.

8. Father, I pray for the restoration of my marriage. Heal the wounds caused by wickedness and bring reconciliation, in Jesus' mighty name.

9. God, give me the patience to persevere through this trial. Help me to trust in your plan and timing, knowing that you are working all things together for my good, in Jesus' mighty name.

10. Lord, I pray for the breaking of generational curses and the establishment of a new legacy of righteousness in my family, in Jesus' mighty name.

## NIGHT PRAYERS

1. Lord, just as you defended Tamar's destiny by removing the wicked men in her life, I pray that you would protect me from the wickedness of my husband and his family, in Jesus' mighty name.

2. Father, I trust that you have a plan for my life, just as you did for Tamar. Give me the strength to endure this difficult season and the faith to believe in your deliverance, in Jesus' mighty name.

3. God, I pray that you would expose the wickedness in my husband's heart, just as you exposed the wickedness of Er and Onan. Bring conviction and repentance, or remove them from my life, in Jesus' mighty name.

4. Lord, I declare that no scheme of the enemy through my husband or his family shall prosper. Defend my destiny, just as you defended Tamar's, in Jesus' mighty name.

5. Heavenly Father, I pray that you would give me favor and vindication, just as you gave Tamar. Let your righteousness prevail in my life and marriage, in Jesus' mighty name.

6. God, I trust in your justice and your timing. I believe that you will fight for me, just as you fought for Tamar, and that you will work all things together for my good, in Jesus' mighty name.

7. Lord, give me the boldness to take a stand for what is right, just as Tamar did. Help me to trust in your protection and provision as I follow your leading, in Jesus' mighty name.

8. Father, I pray that you would redeem my marriage and bring salvation to my husband, just as you redeemed Tamar's story for your purposes. Let your will be done, in Jesus' mighty name.

9. God, I choose to forgive my husband and his family, just as you have forgiven me. Give me the grace to love and pray for them, even in the face of their wickedness, in Jesus' mighty name.

10. Lord, I declare that my destiny is secure in you. No weapon formed against me shall prosper, and every tongue that rises against me in judgment, I shall condemn, just as you vindicated Tamar, in Jesus' mighty name.

## Prayers for deliverance from satanic/occultic families

Scriptures for confession and meditation:

1. "He has delivered us from the power of darkness and conveyed us into the kingdom of the Son of His love." (Colossians 1:13)

2. "Therefore if the Son makes you free, you shall be free indeed." (John 8:36)

3. "For we do not wrestle against flesh and blood, but against principalities, against powers, against the rulers of the darkness of this age, against spiritual hosts of wickedness in the heavenly places." (Ephesians 6:12)

4. "For He has rescued us from the dominion of darkness and brought us into the kingdom of the Son He loves." (Colossians 1:13)

5. "Surely He shall deliver you from the snare of the fowler and from the perilous pestilence." (Psalm 91:3)

6. "And they overcame him by the blood of the Lamb and by the word of their testimony, and they did not love their lives to the death." (Revelation 12:11)

## MORNING PRAYERS

1. Lord, I declare my freedom from any satanic or occultic influences in my family line. I claim deliverance through the power of the blood of Jesus Christ, in Jesus' mighty name.

2. Father, I renounce any and all involvement of my ancestors in the occult. I break every curse and sever every tie with the powers of darkness, in Jesus' mighty name.

3. God, I plead the blood of Jesus over my life and my family. I declare that we are covered and protected by the finished work of Christ on the cross, in Jesus' mighty name.

4. Lord, expose any hidden works of darkness in my family and bring them to light. Shine your truth and dispel every lie of the enemy, in Jesus' mighty name.

5. Heavenly Father, I pray for the salvation of my family members who are still trapped in satanic or occultic practices. Deliver them and set them free, in Jesus' mighty name.

6. God, I declare that no weapon formed against me or my family shall prosper. I cancel every plan and scheme of the enemy against us, in Jesus' mighty name.

7. Lord, send your angels to encamp around me and my loved ones. Protect us from all harm and danger, both physical and spiritual, in Jesus' mighty name.

8. Father, I pray for the healing of any wounds or traumas caused by satanic or occultic influences in my family. Restore us and make us whole, in Jesus' mighty name.

9. God, give me discernment to recognize and resist any attempts of the enemy to infiltrate my life or my family. Help me to stand firm in my faith, in Jesus' mighty name.

10. Lord, I declare that my family and I are children of the light, called out of darkness into your marvelous light. We will walk in the freedom and victory that Christ has won for us, in Jesus' mighty name.

## NIGHT PRAYERS

Prayers:

1. Lord, just as you delivered Tamar from the wickedness of Judah's family, I pray that you would deliver me from any satanic or occultic influences in my family line, in Jesus' mighty name.

2. Father, I plead the blood of Jesus over my life and renounce any covenants or dedications made by my ancestors to darkness. I declare my allegiance to Christ alone, in Jesus' mighty name.

3. God, I pray that you would expose and uproot any hidden works of darkness in my family, just as you exposed the wickedness of Er and Onan. Let your light shine and dispel every shadow, in Jesus' mighty name.

4. Lord, I declare that no generational curse or satanic

assignment shall prosper in my life. I claim my freedom and inheritance in Christ, just as Tamar claimed her rightful place in your plan, in Jesus' mighty name.

5. Heavenly Father, I pray for the salvation and deliverance of my family members who are still bound by satanic or occultic powers. Set them free, just as you set Tamar free from the wickedness of Judah's sons, in Jesus' mighty name.

6. God, I trust in your power to break every chain and shatter every yoke of the enemy. I declare that I am a child of the light, called out of darkness into your marvelous light, just as you called Tamar, in Jesus' mighty name.

7. Lord, give me discernment and wisdom to recognize and resist the schemes of the enemy, just as Tamar discerned the wickedness of her circumstances. Help me to stand firm in my faith, in Jesus' mighty name.

8. Father, I pray for your protection and covering over my life and my family. Surround us with your angels and shield us from every attack of the enemy, in Jesus' mighty name.

9. God, I declare that I will not be ensnared by the lies or temptations of the enemy. I choose to walk in the truth and freedom that Christ has won for me, just as Tamar walked in your truth, in Jesus' mighty name.

10. Lord, I thank you for your delivering power and your unfailing love. I trust that you will lead me into the fullness of my destiny, just as you led Tamar, and that no satanic or occult power shall hinder your plan for my life, in Jesus' mighty name.

## Prayers for protection against wicked in-laws

Scriptures for confession and meditation:

1. "The Lord is my rock and my fortress and my deliverer; my God, my strength, in whom I will trust; my shield and the horn of my salvation, my stronghold." (Psalm 18:2)

2. "Be sober, be vigilant; because your adversary the devil walks about like a roaring lion, seeking whom he may devour. Resist him, steadfast in the faith, knowing that the same sufferings are experienced by your brotherhood in the world." (1 Peter 5:8-9)

3. "The Lord will preserve you from all evil; He will preserve your soul. The Lord will preserve your going out and your coming in from this time forth, and even forevermore." (Psalm 121:7-8)

4. "But the Lord is faithful, who will establish you and guard you from the evil one." (2 Thessalonians 3:3)

5. "The angel of the Lord encamps all around those who fear Him, and delivers them." (Psalm 34:7)

6. "No weapon formed against you shall prosper, and every tongue which rises against you in judgment you shall condemn. This is the heritage of the servants of the Lord, and their righteousness is from Me," says the Lord. (Isaiah 54:17)

MORNING PRAYERS

1. Lord, I pray for your protection against the wickedness of my in-laws. Shield me and my immediate family from their harmful influence, in Jesus' mighty name.

2. Father, give me wisdom and discernment in dealing with my in-laws. Help me to set healthy boundaries and to respond with grace and truth, in Jesus' mighty name.

3. God, I declare that no weapon formed against me by my in-laws shall prosper. I cancel every curse and break every soul tie, in Jesus' mighty name.

4. Lord, expose any hidden agendas or malicious intentions of my in-laws. Bring their deeds into the light and vindicate me, in Jesus' mighty name.

5. Heavenly Father, I pray for the conviction and repentance of my in-laws. Soften their hearts and draw them to your love and truth, in Jesus' mighty name.

6. God, I declare that my home is a sanctuary, protected by the blood of Jesus. No evil influence from my in-laws shall penetrate our dwelling, in Jesus' mighty name.

7. Lord, give me the strength to forgive my in-laws for any harm they have caused. Help me to release bitterness and resentment, and to pray for their salvation, in Jesus' mighty name.

8. Father, I pray for the unity of my marriage and family, despite the interference of wicked in-laws. Bind us together in love and help us to support one another, in Jesus' mighty name.

9. God, I trust in your justice and vengeance. I release my in-laws into your hands, knowing that you will deal with them according to your righteousness, in Jesus' mighty name.

10. Lord, I declare that I am more than a conqueror through Christ who strengthens me. No wickedness of my in-laws shall overcome me, for greater is He that is in me than he that is in the world, in Jesus' mighty name.

## NIGHT PRAYERS

1. Lord, just as you protected Tamar from the wickedness of her father-in-law, Judah, I pray that you would protect me from the wickedness of my in-laws, in Jesus' mighty name.

2. Father, I declare that no weapon formed against me by my in-laws shall prosper. I claim your victory and

your righteousness over every accusation and attack, in Jesus' mighty name.

3. God, I pray that you would give me wisdom and discernment in dealing with my in-laws, just as you gave Tamar wisdom in navigating her difficult circumstances. Help me to respond with grace and truth, in Jesus' mighty name.

4. Lord, expose any hidden agendas or malicious intentions of my in-laws, just as you exposed the wickedness of Judah's sons. Bring their deeds into the light and vindicate me, in Jesus' mighty name.

5. Heavenly Father, I pray for the conviction and repentance of my in-laws, just as Judah was eventually convicted of his own sin. Soften their hearts and draw them to your love and truth, in Jesus' mighty name.

6. God, I declare that my home and my marriage are protected by the blood of Jesus, just as Tamar's destiny was protected by your hand. No scheme or interference of my in-laws shall prosper, in Jesus' mighty name.

7. Lord, give me the strength to forgive my in-laws, just as you have forgiven me. Help me to release bitterness and resentment, and to pray for their salvation, in Jesus' mighty name.

8. Father, I pray for the unity and restoration of my family, despite the opposition of my in-laws. Heal our relationships and bring reconciliation, just as you brought restoration to Tamar's story, in Jesus' mighty name.

9. God, I trust in your justice and your sovereignty. I release my in-laws into your hands, knowing that you will deal with them according to your righteousness, just as you dealt with Judah and his sons, in Jesus'

mighty name.

10. Lord, I declare that I am more than a conqueror through Christ who strengthens me. No weapon of my in-laws shall overtake me, for greater is He that is in me than he that is in the world, just as your purpose prevailed in Tamar's life, in Jesus' mighty name.

## Prayers to redeem your time and fulfill destiny after wasted years

Scriptures for confession and meditation:

1. "So teach us to number our days, that we may gain a heart of wisdom." (Psalm 90:12)

2. "And we know that all things work together for good to those who love God, to those who are the called according to His purpose." (Romans 8:28)

3. "'For I know the thoughts that I think toward you,' says the Lord, 'thoughts of peace and not of evil, to give you a future and a hope.'" (Jeremiah 29:11)

4. "I will restore to you the years that the swarming locust has eaten, the crawling locust, the consuming locust, and the chewing locust, My great army which I sent among you." (Joel 2:25)

5. "And let us not grow weary while doing good, for in due season we shall reap if we do not lose heart." (Galatians 6:9)

6. "Being confident of this very thing, that He who has begun a good work in you will complete it until the day of Jesus Christ." (Philippians 1:6)

MORNING PRAYERS

1. Lord, I ask for Your help and empowerment to redeem the years that have been lost in my life, in Jesus' mighty name.

2. Father, I trust in your ability to restore what the locust

has eaten. I believe that you can take my past mistakes and use them for my good and your glory, in Jesus' mighty name.

3. God, I pray for a renewed sense of purpose and direction in my life. Show me the path you have for me and help me to walk in it with diligence and faith, in Jesus' mighty name.

4. Lord, I declare that my latter days shall be greater than my former days. I believe that you have a plan to prosper me and give me hope, despite my wasted years, in Jesus' mighty name.

5. Heavenly Father, I pray for a fresh anointing of your Holy Spirit upon my life. Renew my strength and give me the grace to pursue my destiny with passion, in Jesus' mighty name.

6. God, I choose to forget the things that are behind and to press forward to the high calling you have for me. Help me to make the most of every opportunity and to live with intention, in Jesus' mighty name.

7. Lord, redeem my time and teach me to number my days. Give me the wisdom to invest in what truly matters and to let go of what doesn't, in Jesus' mighty name.

8. Father, I pray for divine connections and open doors that will help me fulfill my destiny. Bring the right people and opportunities into my life, in Jesus' mighty name.

9. God, I declare that it is never too late to start living the life you have called me to live. I choose to step out in faith and obedience, knowing that you are with me, in Jesus' mighty name.

10. Lord, I thank you that you are the redeemer of time. I trust in your ability to accelerate my progress and

to bring me into the fullness of my destiny, in Jesus' mighty name.

NIGHT PRAYERS:

1. Lord, just as you redeemed Tamar's wasted years and fulfilled her destiny, I pray that you would redeem the time that has been lost in my own life, in Jesus' mighty name.

2. Father, I trust that you can restore what the locust has eaten, just as you restored Tamar's honor and place in your plan. I believe that you can take my past struggles and use them for my good and your glory, in Jesus' mighty name.

3. God, I pray for a fresh vision and purpose for my life, just as you gave Tamar a new purpose in mothering Perez and Zerah. Show me the path you have for me and help me to walk in it with faith and obedience, in Jesus' mighty name.

4. Lord, I declare that my latter days shall be greater than my former days, just as Tamar's latter days were greater than her former days. I believe that you have a plan to prosper me and give me hope, despite my wasted years, in Jesus' mighty name.

5. Heavenly Father, I pray for a fresh anointing of your Holy Spirit upon my life, just as you anointed Tamar for her role in your plan. Renew my strength and give me the grace to pursue my destiny with passion and perseverance, in Jesus' mighty name.

6. God, I choose to forget the pain of my past and to press forward to the high calling you have for me, just as Tamar pressed forward in faith. Help me to make the most of every opportunity and to live with purpose, in Jesus' mighty name.

7. Lord, redeem my time and teach me to number my

days, just as you redeemed Tamar's story in your perfect timing. Give me the wisdom to invest in what truly matters and to let go of what doesn't, in Jesus' mighty name.

8. Father, I pray for divine connections and open doors that will help me fulfill my destiny, just as you divinely orchestrated the events of Tamar's life. Bring the right people and opportunities into my path, in Jesus' mighty name.

9. God, I declare that it is never too late to step into the fullness of my destiny, just as it was not too late for Tamar. I choose to rise up in faith and obedience, knowing that you are with me, in Jesus' mighty name.

10. Lord, I thank you that you are the redeemer of time and the restorer of destiny. I trust in your ability to accelerate my progress and to bring me into the fullness of your plan, just as you did for Tamar, in Jesus' mighty name.

## Prayers of Divine Intervention: Calling on the God of Tamar

1. I am calling upon the God of Tamar, Oh Lord arise and vindicate me.

2. I am calling on the God of Tamar, Oh God arise and break every chain of injustice holding me back.

3. I am calling upon the God of Tamar, Oh Lord arise and restore the years that wickedness has stolen from me.

4. I am calling on the God of Tamar, Oh God arise and turn my mourning into dancing.

5. I am calling upon the God of Tamar, Oh Lord arise and grant me the courage to pursue my rightful destiny.

6. I am calling on the God of Tamar, Oh God arise and expose every hidden agenda against my life.

7. I am calling upon the God of Tamar, Oh Lord arise and bring forth beauty from the ashes of my past.

8. I am calling on the God of Tamar, Oh God arise and make a way where there seems to be no way.

9. I am calling upon the God of Tamar, Oh Lord arise and transform my story into a testimony of Your faithfulness.

10. I am calling on the God of Tamar, Oh God arise and establish my place in Your divine plan.

# CHAPTER 5: RAHAB - FROM HARLOT TO HEROINE

## INTRODUCTION

The story of Rahab, found in the book of Joshua, is a powerful testament to God's grace, mercy, and redemptive power. Rahab, a prostitute living in the city of Jericho, becomes an unlikely hero in the Israelites' conquest of the Promised Land. Her story showcases how God can transform even the most broken and shame-filled past into a beautiful future filled with hope and purpose.

In this chapter, we will explore Rahab's journey from harlot to heroine, highlighting the key moments of her story and the lessons we can learn from her life. We will see how her faith in the God of Israel and her courageous actions not only saved her life but also earned her a place in the lineage of Jesus Christ.

As we delve into Rahab's story, we will discover the transformative power of God's forgiveness and the hope that is available to all, regardless of their past mistakes or present circumstances. We will also examine the importance of faith, obedience, and the willingness to take risks for the sake of God's plan.

The chapter will be structured as follows:

1. The Historical and Cultural Context of Rahab's Story
2. Rahab's Encounter with the Israelite Spies

3. Rahab's Confession of Faith
4. The Scarlet Cord: A Symbol of Salvation
5. Rahab's Deliverance and Inclusion in Israel
6. Rahab's Place in the Lineage of Jesus Christ
7. Lessons from Rahab's Life for Us Today

Following these sections, we will provide a series of heartfelt prayers inspired by Rahab's story. These prayers will be divided into three categories, each addressing a specific need or desire:

a. Prayers to erase the mistakes of your past

b. Prayers for cleansing from sexual sin and indecent lifestyle

c. Prayers for a golden destiny

Each prayer section will include ten prayer points, providing a total of 30 targeted prayers. These prayers will serve as a source of encouragement, hope, and guidance for those who, like Rahab, desire to experience the transformative power of God's grace and redemption in their lives.

Through this chapter, may we be inspired by Rahab's courage, faith, and the way God redeemed her story for His glory. May we find hope in the knowledge that no matter our past or present circumstances, God's love and transformative power are available to us all.

## The Historical and Cultural Context of Rahab's Story

Rahab's story takes place during the time of the Israelites' conquest of Canaan, as recorded in the book of Joshua. The Israelites, under Joshua's leadership, are preparing to enter the Promised Land after their 40-year wilderness journey. Jericho, a heavily fortified city, stands as the first obstacle in their path.

In the ancient Near Eastern culture, Jericho was known for its strategic location and formidable walls. It was also a city steeped in pagan worship and practices, including temple prostitution. Rahab, a resident of Jericho, is identified as a prostitute, reflecting the moral and spiritual decay of the city.

### Rahab's Encounter with the Israelite Spies

As the Israelites prepare to conquer Jericho, Joshua sends two spies to gather intelligence about the city. The spies find lodging in Rahab's house, which is located on the city wall. When the king of Jericho learns of the spies' presence, he sends orders to Rahab to turn them over. However, Rahab chooses to protect the spies, hiding them on her roof and misdirecting the king's men.

Rahab's actions demonstrate her courage and her willingness to take risks for the sake of God's people. Despite her background as a prostitute, she recognizes the God of Israel as the one true God and aligns herself with His purposes.

### Rahab's Confession of Faith

Before helping the spies escape, Rahab makes a powerful confession of faith. She declares to the spies, "I know that the Lord has given you this land and that a great fear of you has fallen on us, so that all who live in this country are melting in fear because of you" (Joshua 2:9). She goes on to acknowledge the God of Israel as "God in heaven above and on the earth below" (Joshua 2:11).

Rahab's confession reveals her growing faith in the God of Israel and her recognition of His power and sovereignty. Despite her pagan background, she embraces the truth of God's supremacy and aligns herself with His people.

### The Scarlet Cord: A Symbol of Salvation

In exchange for her protection, Rahab secures a promise from the spies that they will spare her life and the lives of her family members when the Israelites conquer Jericho. The spies instruct Rahab to tie a scarlet cord in her window as a sign of this agreement, ensuring that she and her family will be saved from destruction.

The scarlet cord becomes a powerful symbol of salvation and redemption. Just as the Israelites were saved from the plague of death by the blood of the Passover lamb, Rahab and her family are spared by the scarlet cord, a reminder of God's mercy and protection.

## Rahab's Deliverance and Inclusion in Israel

When the Israelites conquer Jericho, Rahab and her family are indeed spared, as promised by the spies. The Bible records that "Joshua spared Rahab the prostitute, with her family and all who belonged to her, because she hid the men Joshua had sent as spies to Jericho—and she lives among the Israelites to this day" (Joshua 6:25).

Rahab's deliverance from the destruction of Jericho marks a turning point in her life. She is not only spared physically but also spiritually, as she is welcomed into the community of Israel. Her story becomes a powerful testament to God's grace and His willingness to redeem and transform even the most unlikely of individuals.

## Rahab's Place in the Lineage of Jesus Christ

Rahab's story does not end with her deliverance from Jericho. In a remarkable turn of events, she goes on to marry Salmon, a member of the tribe of Judah, and becomes the mother of Boaz, who later marries Ruth. Through this lineage, Rahab becomes an ancestor of King David and, ultimately, of Jesus Christ (Matthew 1:5).

Rahab's inclusion in the lineage of the Messiah is a powerful reminder of God's redemptive purposes and His ability to use even the most broken and unlikely individuals for His glory. Her story becomes a testament to the transformative power of faith and the far-reaching impact of God's grace.

## Lessons from Rahab's Life for Us Today

Rahab's story offers valuable lessons and insights for our lives today:

1. God's grace extends to all: Rahab's story reminds us that no one is beyond the reach of God's grace and

redemption. Regardless of our past or our present circumstances, God's love and forgiveness are available to all who turn to Him in faith.

2. Faith is demonstrated through action: Rahab's faith was not merely intellectual assent; it was demonstrated through her courageous actions in protecting the spies and aligning herself with God's purposes. Our faith, too, should be lived out through obedience and tangible acts of love and service.

3. God can use anyone for His purposes: Rahab's story showcases God's ability to use unlikely individuals for His glory. No matter our background, our limitations, or our failures, God can redeem our stories and use us for His purposes when we surrender our lives to Him.

4. Our past does not define our future: Rahab's past as a prostitute did not disqualify her from being used by God or from experiencing His redemption. In Christ, our past mistakes and sins do not define us; instead, we are given a new identity and a hope-filled future.

5. Salvation is available to all who believe: Just as Rahab and her family were saved by faith, symbolized by the scarlet cord, we too can experience salvation through faith in Jesus Christ. His sacrificial death on the cross extends the offer of redemption to all who believe.

As we reflect on Rahab's story, may we be encouraged by the transformative power of God's grace and inspired to live out our faith with courage and obedience. May we trust in His ability to redeem our stories and use us for His glory, no matter our past or present circumstances.

## Prayers to Erase the Mistakes of Your Past

1. Gracious Father, I come before You today with a heart heavy with the weight of my past mistakes. Like Rahab, I have made choices that have left me feeling

ashamed and unworthy. But I know that Your love and mercy are greater than my deepest regrets. I ask that You would wash me clean and erase the stains of my past, making me new in Your sight. In Jesus' name, Amen.

2. Merciful God, I confess that I have often allowed my past mistakes to define me and hold me back from embracing the future You have for me. I pray that You would help me to let go of the shame and guilt that cling to me, and to instead cling to Your promise of forgiveness and redemption. Help me to see myself as You see me - a beloved child, worthy of Your grace and mercy. In Jesus' name, Amen.

3. Loving Savior, I thank You for the power of Your blood, shed on the cross for the forgiveness of my sins. I pray that You would apply that precious blood to the mistakes of my past, erasing them from my record and my memory. Help me to walk in the freedom and newness of life that You have purchased for me. In Jesus' name, Amen.

4. Compassionate Father, I acknowledge that my past mistakes have not only affected me but also those around me. I pray for the healing and restoration of any relationships that have been damaged by my actions. I ask that You would give me the courage to seek forgiveness and reconciliation, and to trust in Your power to redeem and restore what has been broken. In Jesus' name, Amen.

5. Mighty God, I pray that You would replace the painful memories of my past with the truth of Your love and the hope of Your promises. Help me to fix my eyes on the future You have for me, rather than dwelling on the mistakes of yesterday. Give me the strength to press forward into the abundant life You have prepared for

me. In Jesus' name, Amen.

6. Gracious Redeemer, I thank You for the examples in Your Word of those who, like Rahab, have found redemption and purpose despite their past mistakes. I pray that You would use my story, my testimony of Your grace, to bring hope and encouragement to others who are struggling under the weight of their own regrets. May my life be a living testament to Your transformative power. In Jesus' name, Amen.

7. Loving Father, I pray that You would help me to extend to myself the same grace and forgiveness that You have extended to me. Help me to silence the voice of the accuser who would seek to keep me bound by my past, and to instead listen to Your voice of love and acceptance. Teach me to embrace the new identity I have in You. In Jesus' name, Amen.

8. Merciful Savior, I pray that You would give me the wisdom and discernment to learn from my past mistakes, rather than being defined by them. Help me to use the lessons I have learned to make better choices and to walk in obedience to Your will. May my past be a testimony of Your redemptive power and a foundation for a brighter future. In Jesus' name, Amen.

9. Compassionate God, I lift up to You the deep wounds and scars that my past mistakes have left on my heart and soul. I pray that You would bring Your healing touch to these places of pain, replacing them with Your peace, joy, and wholeness. Help me to trust in Your power to restore and redeem even the most broken parts of my story. In Jesus' name, Amen.

10. Faithful Father, I thank You for Your unchanging love and Your unending mercy. I praise You for the promise that, no matter my past mistakes, Your plans for me are good and filled with hope. I surrender my past,

present, and future into Your loving hands, trusting in Your power to erase my mistakes and lead me into the glorious destiny You have prepared for me. In Jesus' name, Amen.

## Prayers for Cleansing from Sexual Sin and Indecent Lifestyle

1. Merciful Father, I come before You today with a heavy heart, burdened by the weight of my sexual sins and indecent lifestyle. Like Rahab, I have strayed from Your path of purity and righteousness, but I know that Your love and forgiveness are greater than my deepest failures. I pray that You would wash me clean, purifying my heart, mind, and body from the stains of my sin. In Jesus' name, Amen.

2. Holy God, I confess that I have often allowed the desires of my flesh to control me, leading me into sexual sin and an indecent lifestyle. I pray that You would break the power of these sinful patterns in my life, setting me free from the bondage of temptation and addiction. Help me to walk in the freedom and holiness that You have called me to. In Jesus' name, Amen.

3. Loving Savior, I thank You for the power of Your blood, shed on the cross for the forgiveness of my sins. I pray that You would apply that precious blood to my life, cleansing me from the guilt and shame of my sexual sins. Help me to receive Your forgiveness and to walk in the newness of life that You have purchased for me. In Jesus' name, Amen.

4. Gracious Father, I acknowledge that my sexual sins and indecent lifestyle have not only affected me but also those around me. I pray for the healing and restoration of any relationships that have been damaged by my actions. I ask that You would give me the courage to

seek accountability, support, and wise counsel as I seek to walk in purity and righteousness. In Jesus' name, Amen.

5. Mighty God, I pray that You would renew my mind and transform my thoughts, replacing any impure or indecent desires with a hunger and thirst for righteousness. Help me to fill my mind with things that are true, noble, right, pure, lovely, and admirable, so that my life may reflect the beauty of Your holiness. In Jesus' name, Amen.

6. Merciful Redeemer, I thank You for the examples in Your Word of those who, like Rahab, have found forgiveness and redemption from their past sins. I pray that You would use my story of transformation to bring hope and encouragement to others who are struggling with sexual sin and an indecent lifestyle. May my life be a testimony of Your power to restore and redeem. In Jesus' name, Amen.

7. Loving Father, I pray that You would help me to embrace my identity as Your beloved child, created in Your image and called to a life of purity and righteousness. Help me to resist the lies of the enemy who would seek to define me by my past sins, and to instead stand firm in the truth of who I am in Christ. In Jesus' name, Amen.

8. Holy Spirit, I invite You to fill me afresh with Your presence and power. I pray that You would give me the strength to flee from sexual temptation and to pursue a lifestyle of holiness and integrity. Help me to be quick to repent and turn back to You whenever I stumble or fall. In Jesus' name, Amen.

9. Compassionate God, I lift up to You the deep wounds and scars that my sexual sins have left on my heart, mind, and body. I pray that You would bring Your

healing touch to these places of pain, replacing them with Your peace, wholeness, and restoration. Help me to trust in Your power to redeem even the most broken parts of my story. In Jesus' name, Amen.

10. Faithful Father, I thank You for Your unwavering love and Your abundant grace. I praise You for the promise that, no matter my past sins, Your plans for me are good and filled with hope. I surrender my life into Your loving hands, trusting in Your power to cleanse me, restore me, and lead me into a future of purity, righteousness, and joy. In Jesus' name, Amen.

## Prayers for a Golden Destiny

1. Gracious Father, I come before You today with a heart full of hope and expectation. I believe that, like Rahab, You have a golden destiny planned for me, a future filled with purpose, joy, and significance. I pray that You would guide my steps and lead me into the fullness of all that You have prepared for me. In Jesus' name, Amen.

2. Mighty God, I acknowledge that You are the author and perfecter of my faith, the one who holds my destiny in Your loving hands. I pray that You would give me the courage and faith to trust in Your plans for my life, even when the path ahead seems uncertain or challenging. Help me to hold fast to Your promises and to walk in obedience to Your will. In Jesus' name, Amen.

3. Loving Savior, I thank You for the price You paid on the cross to secure my eternal destiny. I pray that You would help me to live each day in light of that destiny, pursuing a life that honors You and reflects Your glory. Give me a heart that seeks first Your kingdom and Your righteousness. In Jesus' name, Amen.

4. Wise Father, I pray that You would give me the wisdom

and discernment to make choices that align with the golden destiny You have for me. Help me to seek Your guidance in every decision, big or small, and to trust in Your leading. May my life be a testament to the goodness and faithfulness of Your plans. In Jesus' name, Amen.

5. Merciful God, I confess that there are times when I feel unworthy or inadequate to pursue the golden destiny You have for me. I pray that You would remind me of my true identity in Christ, and that You would fill me with the confidence and strength that comes from knowing I am Your beloved child. Help me to embrace the unique gifts and callings You have placed within me. In Jesus' name, Amen.

6. Sovereign Lord, I recognize that my golden destiny is not just about me, but about the impact I can have on others for Your kingdom. I pray that You would use me as a vessel of Your love, mercy, and truth, bringing hope and transformation to those around me. Help me to be a faithful steward of the destiny You have entrusted to me. In Jesus' name, Amen.

7. Gracious Redeemer, I thank You for the examples in Your Word of those who, like Rahab, have stepped into the golden destiny You had for them, despite their past or their circumstances. I pray that You would give me the faith and courage to do the same, trusting in Your power to redeem and restore all things. May my life be a living testimony of Your transformative grace. In Jesus' name, Amen.

8. Holy Spirit, I invite You to fill me afresh with Your presence and power, equipping me to pursue the golden destiny God has for me. I pray that You would give me the strength to persevere through challenges and obstacles, the wisdom to discern Your leading, and

the passion to chase after Your purposes with all my heart. In Jesus' name, Amen.

9. Loving Father, I pray that You would surround me with people who will support, encourage, and challenge me as I pursue my golden destiny. Bring mentors, friends, and partners into my life who will help me to grow in faith, character, and obedience to Your will. May we spur one another on toward love and good deeds. In Jesus' name, Amen.

10. Faithful God, I thank You for Your unwavering commitment to my life and to the golden destiny You have for me. I praise You for Your goodness, Your faithfulness, and Your unfailing love. I surrender my life into Your loving hands, trusting in Your power to lead me into the glorious future You have prepared for me. May my life bring honor and glory to Your name, now and forever. In Jesus' name, Amen.

# CHAPTER 6: RUTH – A STORY OF REDEMPTION

## INTRODUCTION

The story of Ruth is a beautiful testament to God's redeeming love and His ability to transform lives and destinies. Set in the time of the judges, this narrative showcases the journey of a young Moabite widow who, through her devotion and faithfulness, finds herself grafted into the lineage of Jesus Christ.

In this chapter, we will explore the various aspects of redemption woven throughout Ruth's story. We will examine the role of Boaz as the kinsman-redeemer, who selflessly steps in to rescue Ruth and Naomi from their desperate circumstances. We will also highlight the redemption of Naomi, who, through Ruth's love and dedication, finds her bitterness transformed into joy and her emptiness filled with new life.

As we delve into the lives of these women, we will discover powerful lessons about God's sovereignty, His love for the outsider, and His ability to redeem even the most hopeless of situations. We will see how Ruth's foreign status did not hinder God's plan for her life, but rather became a testament to His inclusive love and grace.

The chapter will be structured as follows:

1. The Context of Ruth's Story

2. Naomi and Ruth: A Journey from Emptiness to Fullness
3. Boaz: The Kinsman-Redeemer
4. The Unnamed Relative: A Contrast in Character
5. Ruth's Redemption: From Widow to Wife
6. Naomi's Redemption: The Power of Love and Loyalty
7. The Significance of Ruth's Lineage
8. Lessons from Ruth's Story for Our Lives Today

Following these sections, we will provide a series of heartfelt prayers inspired by Ruth's story. These prayers will be divided into three categories, each addressing a specific need or situation:

a. Prayers for widows

b. Prayers for women in foreign countries/cultures hoping to be married

c. Prayers for destiny redemption

Each prayer section will include ten prayer points for both morning and night, providing a total of 60 targeted prayers. These prayers will serve as a source of comfort, encouragement, and hope for those who find themselves in circumstances similar to Ruth and Naomi, reminding them of God's unfailing love and His power to redeem and restore.

Through this chapter, may we be inspired by Ruth's courage, faith, and devotion, and may we find hope in the knowledge that our God is a God of redemption, who can transform even the darkest of circumstances into a beautiful tapestry of His grace and purpose.

**The Context of Ruth's Story**

To fully appreciate the depth and significance of Ruth's story, it is essential to understand the historical and cultural context in which it takes place. The events of the Book of Ruth occur during the time of the judges, a turbulent period in Israel's history marked by political instability, moral decline, and spiritual apostasy.

Against this backdrop, we are introduced to Naomi, a woman from Bethlehem who, due to a severe famine, emigrates with her husband and two sons to the land of Moab. Tragically, Naomi's husband dies, and her sons marry Moabite women, Orpah and Ruth. After about ten years, both of Naomi's sons also die, leaving her alone with her daughters-in-law in a foreign land.

It is important to note that Moabites were considered outsiders and were often viewed with suspicion and prejudice by the Israelites. This cultural divide adds an additional layer of complexity to Ruth's story, as her loyalty to Naomi and her decision to embrace the God of Israel would have been seen as remarkable and counter-cultural.

**Naomi and Ruth: A Journey from Emptiness to Fullness**

The story of Ruth begins with a poignant picture of emptiness and loss. Naomi, having lost her husband and sons, decides to return to her homeland of Bethlehem, believing that the Lord has dealt bitterly with her. She encourages her daughters-in-law to return to their own families, but Ruth refuses to leave Naomi's side, declaring, "Where you go I will go, and where you stay I will stay. Your people will be my people and your God my God" (Ruth 1:16).

Ruth's dedication to Naomi is a powerful example of hesed, the Hebrew word for steadfast love and loyalty. Despite the uncertainty of her future as a widowed foreigner, Ruth chooses to cling to Naomi and to the God of Israel, trusting that He will provide for and guide them.

As the story unfolds, we witness God's hand at work in the lives of these women, gradually filling their emptiness with new hope and purpose. Through Ruth's faithfulness and the kindness of Boaz, Naomi's bitterness is transformed into joy, and her life is infused with new meaning and fulfilment.

## Boaz: The Kinsman-Redeemer

Boaz, a wealthy relative of Naomi's late husband, emerges as a central figure in the story of Ruth's redemption. As Ruth goes out to glean in the fields to provide for herself and Naomi, she finds herself working in a field belonging to Boaz. Boaz takes notice of Ruth and, having heard of her devotion to Naomi, shows her favor and kindness, ensuring her protection and provision.

As the narrative progresses, it becomes clear that Boaz is more than just a generous benefactor; he is a kinsman-redeemer. In Israelite society, the kinsman-redeemer was a close relative who had the responsibility to rescue and restore the family of a deceased relative, which included marrying the widow to provide an heir and preserve the family line.

Boaz, in his role as kinsman-redeemer, demonstrates the characteristics of a true redeemer: compassion, generosity, and a willingness to put the needs of others above his own. He goes above and beyond in his care for Ruth and Naomi, ultimately taking on the role of husband to Ruth and father to their child, thus securing their future and redeeming their story.

## The Unnamed Relative: A Contrast in Character

Before Boaz can fully step into his role as Ruth's kinsman-redeemer, he must first address the claim of a closer relative who has the first right of redemption. This unnamed relative, when presented with the opportunity to redeem Ruth and Naomi's property, initially expresses interest. However, upon learning that redeeming the property would also involve marrying Ruth and potentially endangering his own inheritance, the relative declines, stating, "I cannot redeem it because I might endanger my own estate" (Ruth 4:6).

The actions of this unnamed relative stand in stark contrast to those of Boaz. While the relative is concerned with protecting his own interests and assets, Boaz willingly takes on the responsibility of redeeming Ruth and Naomi, even at the potential cost to himself. This contrast serves to highlight the selflessness and integrity of Boaz and emphasizes the true nature of redemption, which often requires sacrifice and putting the needs of others before one's own.

**Ruth's Redemption: From Widow to Wife**

Through the selfless actions of Boaz, Ruth's story takes a remarkable turn. The once widowed and destitute foreigner becomes the wife of a respected and influential man in Bethlehem. Ruth's redemption is not only a personal victory but also a powerful testament to God's love and acceptance of all people, regardless of their background or status.

Ruth's journey from widow to wife also serves as a beautiful analogy for the redemptive work of Christ. Just as Boaz redeemed Ruth from her desperate circumstances and welcomed her into his family, Jesus Christ, our ultimate Redeemer, rescues us from the bondage of sin and grafts us into His eternal family.

**Naomi's Redemption: The Power of Love and Loyalty**

While the story of Ruth often focuses on the young Moabite woman, the redemption of Naomi is equally significant. Through Ruth's unwavering love and loyalty, Naomi's life is transformed from one of bitterness and emptiness to one of joy and abundance.

The women of Bethlehem recognize the depth of Ruth's devotion to Naomi, declaring, "Your daughter-in-law, who loves you and who is better to you than seven sons, has given him birth" (Ruth 4:15). In a society where sons were highly valued, this statement is a powerful affirmation of the worth and impact of Ruth's presence in Naomi's life.

Naomi's redemption serves as a reminder that God's love and providence can reach us through the most unexpected sources. It also highlights the transformative power of hesed, the steadfast love and loyalty exemplified by Ruth, which has the ability to heal wounds, restore hope, and bring new life to even the most broken of circumstances.

## The Significance of Ruth's Lineage

The story of Ruth culminates in a powerful revelation of her lineage. Ruth and Boaz's son, Obed, becomes the father of Jesse, who is the father of King David. This places Ruth, a Moabite woman, in the direct lineage of not only Israel's greatest king but also of Jesus Christ, the Messiah.

The inclusion of Ruth in the lineage of Jesus is a remarkable testament to God's sovereign plan and His love for all people. It demonstrates that God's purposes are not limited by human prejudices or cultural barriers and that He can use even the most unlikely individuals to fulfill His divine will.

Ruth's story also serves as a beautiful foreshadowing of the inclusive nature of the gospel message. Just as Ruth, a foreigner, was welcomed into the family of God, the gospel extends God's love and redemption to all people, regardless of their ethnicity, background, or past.

## Lessons from Ruth's Story for Our Lives Today

The story of Ruth is rich with lessons and insights that remain relevant for our lives today. Here are a few key takeaways:

1. God's love and redemption are available to all: Ruth's story reminds us that God's love and redemptive power are not limited by our background, nationality, or social status. He welcomes all who seek Him into His family.

2. Loyalty and devotion are powerful forces: Ruth's unwavering loyalty to Naomi and her faith in the God of Israel serve as an example of the transformative power of hesed, steadfast love and devotion. When we commit ourselves to loving God and others selflessly, we open the door for incredible blessings and redemption.

3. God can use our trials for His purposes: The hardships and losses experienced by Ruth and Naomi were not wasted. God used their difficult circumstances to bring about a beautiful story of redemption and to fulfill His purposes. We can trust that God is able to work through our own trials and challenges to bring about His good plans.

4. Redemption often requires sacrifice: Boaz's willingness to sacrifice his own interests and resources to redeem Ruth and Naomi reflects the sacrificial nature of true redemption. As followers of Christ, we are called to live lives of sacrificial love, putting the needs of others before our own.

5. God's plans are greater than our limitations: Ruth's story demonstrates that God's purposes are not hindered by human limitations or expectations. He can use unlikely people and circumstances to bring about His will and to further His kingdom.

As we reflect on the story of Ruth, may we be inspired to live lives characterized by faith, devotion, and openness to God's redemptive work in and through us. May we trust in His sovereign plan and love for us, knowing that He is able to redeem even the most challenging of circumstances for His glory and our good.

## Prayers for Widows

*Morning Prayers*

1. Loving Father, I come before You today as a widow, feeling the weight of my loss and the challenges that lie ahead. I thank You for Your promise to be a defender of widows and to uplift those who are bowed down. I ask for Your strength, comfort, and guidance as I navigate this season of my life. In Jesus' name, Amen.

2. Compassionate God, You see the depths of my pain and

the loneliness that often overwhelms me. I pray that You would be my constant companion, my source of hope and peace. Help me to find joy in Your presence and to trust in Your unfailing love, even in the midst of my grief. In Jesus' name, Amen.

3. Gracious Lord, I thank You for the precious memories of my spouse and the love we shared. As I face the daily challenges of life without them, I ask for Your wisdom and discernment in making decisions and caring for my family. Help me to lean on Your understanding and to trust in Your provision. In Jesus' name, Amen.

4. Mighty God, I pray for the strength and resilience to face each day with courage and faith. When I feel overwhelmed by the responsibilities and burdens I now bear alone, remind me that You are my ever-present help and that I can do all things through Christ who gives me strength. In Jesus' name, Amen.

5. Loving Father, I pray for the grace to forgive those who may have wronged or abandoned me in my time of need. Help me to release any bitterness or resentment and to extend compassion and understanding, just as You have shown me. May I find healing and freedom in Your love. In Jesus' name, Amen.

6. Compassionate God, I lift up other widows who are struggling with loneliness, financial hardship, or the challenges of single parenthood. I pray that You would be their comfort, their provider, and their source of strength. Surround them with a supportive community and remind them of Your constant presence and care. In Jesus' name, Amen.

7. Gracious Lord, I thank You for the promise of new beginnings and the hope that is found in You. Help me to embrace the opportunities for growth and service that this season of life may bring. Use me as a vessel of

Your love and comfort to other widows and those who are hurting. In Jesus' name, Amen.

8. Mighty God, I pray for the wisdom and guidance to steward my resources well and to make wise choices for my future. Help me to trust in Your provision and to find my security in You alone. Give me the faith to step out into new adventures and to embrace the plans You have for me. In Jesus' name, Amen.

9. Loving Father, I pray for the healing of my heart and the restoration of my joy. When waves of grief threaten to overwhelm me, remind me of Your steadfast love and the eternal hope I have in You. Help me to find moments of laughter, beauty, and connection, even in the midst of my pain. In Jesus' name, Amen.

10. Compassionate God, I thank You for the promise that You will never leave or forsake me. As I face the uncertainties of the future, I pray that You would be my constant companion, my guide, and my source of peace. Help me to lean on Your strength and to find my hope in You alone. In Jesus' name, Amen.

*Evening Prayers*

1. Gracious Lord, as I come to the end of another day, I thank You for Your faithfulness and the comfort of Your presence. I lay my burdens and sorrows at Your feet, trusting in Your promise to give rest to the weary and to carry our heavy loads. May I find peace and restoration in You tonight. In Jesus' name, Amen.

2. Loving Father, I confess the times when I have allowed fear, worry, or bitterness to take root in my heart. I pray that You would grant me the grace to release these burdens and to entrust my life and future into Your capable hands. Help me to find my security and identity in You alone. In Jesus' name, Amen.

3. Compassionate God, I pray for the strength and perseverance to face the ongoing challenges of widowhood. When loneliness creeps in or the weight of responsibility feels overwhelming, remind me that You are my ever-present help and that Your grace is sufficient for every need. In Jesus' name, Amen.

4. Mighty God, I pray for the protection of my heart, mind, and home. Guard me against the schemes of the enemy and the temptations that may arise in moments of vulnerability. Surround me with Your peace and help me to find my refuge in You. In Jesus' name, Amen.

5. Gracious Lord, I thank You for the gift of community and the love and support of friends and family. I pray that You would continue to bring people into my life who can offer encouragement, understanding, and practical help. May I also be a source of comfort and strength to others who are hurting. In Jesus' name, Amen.

6. Loving Father, I pray for the grace to forgive myself for any regrets, guilt, or self-blame I may be harboring in relation to my spouse's passing. Help me to embrace the freedom and healing that is found in Your love and to trust in Your redemptive power to bring beauty from ashes. In Jesus' name, Amen.

7. Compassionate God, I lift up the needs and concerns of my family to You. I pray that You would bring healing to strained relationships, provide for financial needs, and guide my children in their own journeys of faith. Help me to be a source of love, wisdom, and support for those entrusted to my care. In Jesus' name, Amen.

8. Mighty God, I pray for the wisdom and discernment to navigate the practical aspects of widowhood, such as managing finances, making important decisions, and caring for my home. Grant me the clarity and

confidence to seek help when needed and to trust in Your guidance every step of the way. In Jesus' name, Amen.

9. Gracious Lord, I thank You for the hope of eternal life and the promise of reunion with loved ones in Your presence. When my heart aches with the pain of separation, I pray that You would comfort me with the assurance of Your eternal love and the joy that awaits in Heaven. Help me to live each day with the perspective of eternity and to find hope in Your unfailing promises. In Jesus' name, Amen.

10. Loving Father, as I lay down to sleep, I entrust my life and my future into Your loving hands. I pray that You would guard my heart and mind with Your perfect peace and that I would awaken with a renewed sense of Your presence and purpose for my life. May I find rest and restoration in You tonight. In Jesus' name, Amen.

## Prayers to be remarried

*Morning Prayers*

1. Gracious Lord, just as You brought Boaz into Ruth's life, I pray that You would bring my own Boaz - a godly, loving, and compassionate spouse - into my life. Guide our paths to cross and help us to recognize Your divine orchestration in our meeting. In Jesus' name, Amen.

2. Loving Father, I trust in Your perfect plan and timing for my life, including my desire for remarriage. I pray that You would prepare my heart and the heart of my future spouse for the covenant of marriage, and that You would bring us together in Your appointed time. In Jesus' name, Amen.

3. Mighty God, I pray for the wisdom and discernment to recognize the qualities of a godly spouse, just as Boaz demonstrated kindness, integrity, and faithfulness.

Help me to trust in Your provision and to wait upon Your timing, knowing that You have my best interests at heart. In Jesus' name, Amen.

4. Compassionate God, I lift up any past hurts, disappointments, or fears that may be hindering my ability to fully trust and open my heart to the possibility of remarriage. I pray for Your healing touch and the power of Your redeeming love to restore and renew my hope in love and marriage. In Jesus' name, Amen.

5. Gracious Lord, I pray that You would be preparing and shaping my future spouse, even now. Help them to grow in their faith, character, and love for You, and to be ready to enter into the sacred covenant of marriage. Bring us together in Your perfect timing and way. In Jesus' name, Amen.

6. Loving Father, I thank You for Your faithfulness and Your promise to provide for all my needs, including my desire for a godly spouse. I trust in Your love and Your ability to bring beauty from ashes, just as You did in the story of Ruth and Boaz. Help me to rest in Your perfect peace. In Jesus' name, Amen.

7. Mighty God, I pray for the courage and faith to step out in obedience, just as Ruth did when she approached Boaz. Help me to trust in Your leading and to be open to the opportunities and relationships that You bring into my life, knowing that You are guiding my every step. In Jesus' name, Amen.

8. Compassionate God, I lift up my future spouse and pray for Your blessing, protection, and guidance over their life. Prepare their heart for the commitment and covenant of marriage, and help them to seek Your will above all else. Bring us together in Your perfect love and timing. In Jesus' name, Amen.

9. Gracious Lord, I pray for the patience and contentment to wait upon Your timing for remarriage, trusting that Your plans for me are good and filled with hope. Help me to find my fulfillment and joy in You, and to use this season of singleness to grow in my faith and relationship with You. In Jesus' name, Amen.

10. Loving Father, I thank You for the hope and promise of redemption, both in my life and in my future marriage. I trust in Your ability to write a beautiful love story, just as You did for Ruth and Boaz. Help me to keep my eyes fixed on You and to trust in Your perfect plan for my life. In Jesus' name, Amen.

*Evening Prayers*

1. Heavenly Father, I come before You with a heart longing for a godly spouse. Just as You orchestrated the events that brought Ruth and Boaz together, I trust in Your divine plan for my life. Guide my path and lead me to the person You have chosen for me. In Jesus' name, Amen.

2. Gracious God, I pray for the strength and resilience to trust in Your timing, even when the wait seems long. Help me to find contentment and purpose in this season of singleness, and to use this time to cultivate a deeper relationship with You. Prepare my heart for the blessing of remarriage. In Jesus' name, Amen.

3. Loving Lord, I ask that You would bring a God-fearing and compassionate spouse into my life, just as Boaz was to Ruth. Give me the wisdom to recognize the qualities of a godly partner and the discernment to know when You are leading me towards marriage. In Jesus' name, Amen.

4. Mighty Redeemer, I pray that You would heal any wounds or fears that may be hindering my ability to fully embrace the possibility of remarriage. Help me to

release any past disappointments or hurts, and to trust in Your power to restore and redeem my story. In Jesus' name, Amen.

5. Faithful God, I thank You for Your steadfast love and Your promise to provide for all my needs. I trust that You are working behind the scenes, preparing my future spouse and orchestrating our meeting. Help me to wait patiently and expectantly for Your perfect timing. In Jesus' name, Amen.

6. Gracious Father, I pray that You would surround me with supportive and encouraging people who will uplift me in my journey towards remarriage. Bring wise counsel and godly examples into my life, and help me to seek Your guidance in all my relationships. In Jesus' name, Amen.

7. Loving Savior, I ask that You would guard my heart and mind as I navigate the path towards remarriage. Protect me from any deception or temptation, and help me to stay anchored in Your truth. Give me the discernment to make wise choices and to honor You in all my relationships. In Jesus' name, Amen.

8. Mighty God, I pray for the faith and courage to take steps of obedience, even when the way seems unclear. Just as Ruth trusted in Your provision and stepped out in faith, help me to trust in Your guidance and to follow Your leading in my pursuit of a godly spouse. In Jesus' name, Amen.

9. Compassionate Lord, I lift up my future spouse to You, wherever they may be. I pray that You would be drawing them closer to Yourself, preparing their heart for the covenant of marriage, and leading them on a path towards me. Bring us together in Your perfect love and timing. In Jesus' name, Amen.

10. Gracious Redeemer, I thank You for Your faithfulness

and Your ability to write beautiful stories of redemption and love. I trust in Your plans for my life, including my desire for remarriage. Help me to fix my eyes on You, to find my joy in Your presence, and to trust in Your perfect orchestration of my love story. In Jesus' name, Amen.

## Prayers for Women in Foreign Countries/Cultures Hoping to Be Married
*Morning Prayers*

1. Gracious Lord, I come before You today as a woman living in a foreign country, longing for the blessing of marriage. I trust in Your perfect plan for my life and ask that You would guide me in this journey, aligning my heart's desires with Your will. Give me the patience and faith to wait upon Your timing. In Jesus' name, Amen.

2. Loving Father, I thank You for the beauty and richness of the culture in which I find myself. As I navigate the challenges and opportunities of living in a foreign land, I pray that You would grant me wisdom, understanding, and a deep sense of belonging. Help me to find my identity and security in You. In Jesus' name, Amen.

3. Mighty God, I pray for the breaking down of any cultural barriers or prejudices that may hinder my ability to form meaningful relationships and connections. Help me to extend love, grace, and understanding to those around me and to be a bridge-builder in my community. In Jesus' name, Amen.

4. Compassionate God, I lift up the desire of my heart for a loving and godly spouse. I pray that You would be preparing and guiding my future husband, even now, and that our paths would cross in Your perfect timing. Give me the discernment to recognize Your leading and

the courage to trust in Your provision. In Jesus' name, Amen.

5. Gracious Lord, I pray for the strength and resilience to face any loneliness, homesickness, or feelings of isolation that may arise as I navigate life in a foreign culture. Remind me that You are my constant companion and that I am never truly alone. Surround me with a supportive community and deep friendships. In Jesus' name, Amen.

6. Loving Father, I ask for Your protection and guidance in my interactions with men in this culture. Give me the wisdom to set appropriate boundaries and to honor You in my relationships. Guard my heart and mind from temptation or compromise and help me to trust in Your perfect love. In Jesus' name, Amen.

7. Mighty God, I pray for opportunities to grow in my faith and to deepen my relationship with You during this season of singleness. Help me to use this time to cultivate a heart of service, compassion, and devotion to You. Prepare me to be a godly wife and partner in the future. In Jesus' name, Amen.

8. Compassionate God, I lift up other women in foreign cultures who share my desire for marriage. I pray that You would encourage their hearts, strengthen their faith, and provide for their needs. Help us to support and uplift one another in our journeys and to trust in Your perfect plan. In Jesus' name, Amen.

9. Gracious Lord, I pray for the grace to embrace the unique experiences and growth opportunities that come with living in a foreign culture. Help me to learn from the people and customs around me and to appreciate the beauty in diversity. Use this time to shape me into the woman You have called me to be. In Jesus' name, Amen.

10. Loving Father, I thank You for the promise that You are working all things together for my good and that Your plans for me are filled with hope and a future. As I trust in You and seek Your will, I pray that You would lead me to the spouse You have chosen for me and that our union would bring glory to Your name. In Jesus' name, Amen.

*Evening Prayers*

1. Gracious Lord, as I come to the end of another day, I thank You for Your faithfulness and loving presence in my life. I lay my hopes, dreams, and longings for marriage at Your feet, trusting in Your perfect timing and provision. Give me the peace and contentment that comes from resting in Your love. In Jesus' name, Amen.

2. Loving Father, I confess any times when I have allowed fear, doubt, or impatience to cloud my vision of Your plan for my life. I pray that You would renew my faith and trust in Your goodness and that I would find my joy and fulfillment in You alone. Help me to surrender my desires to Your perfect will. In Jesus' name, Amen.

3. Mighty God, I pray for the strength and wisdom to navigate any cultural differences or challenges that may arise as I seek to build relationships and connections in this foreign land. Help me to approach others with empathy, respect, and a Christ-like love that transcends all barriers. In Jesus' name, Amen.

4. Compassionate God, I lift up any feelings of loneliness, disappointment, or frustration that may arise in my journey towards marriage. I pray that You would comfort my heart, renew my hope, and remind me of Your constant presence and unfailing love. Help me to find contentment and purpose in You. In Jesus' name, Amen.

5. Gracious Lord, I thank You for the gift of community and the support of friends, family, and fellow believers. I pray that You would continue to surround me with people who encourage my faith, offer godly wisdom, and provide a sense of belonging in this foreign culture. May I also be a source of light and love to those around me. In Jesus' name, Amen.

6. Loving Father, I pray for the grace to trust in Your sovereignty and to release any control I may be trying to maintain over my journey towards marriage. Help me to embrace the adventures, lessons, and opportunities for growth that this season of singleness may bring, knowing that You are directing my steps. In Jesus' name, Amen.

7. Mighty God, I pray for the protection of my heart, mind, and body as I navigate the complexities of relationships and cultural expectations. Guard me against any temptations or compromises that may arise and help me to honor You in all my interactions with others. Give me the discernment to make wise choices. In Jesus' name, Amen.

8. Compassionate God, I lift up the men in this culture, both believers and non-believers. I pray that You would be working in their hearts, drawing them to a deeper understanding of Your love and truth. Prepare the heart of my future spouse to be a godly leader, provider, and partner. In Jesus' name, Amen.

9. Gracious Lord, I thank You for the examples of godly marriages and relationships that You have placed in my life. I pray that You would use these models to inspire and encourage me in my own journey and that I would learn from their wisdom and experiences. Help me to trust in Your perfect design for marriage. In Jesus' name, Amen.

10. Loving Father, as I lay down to sleep, I entrust my dreams, hopes, and future into Your loving hands. I pray that You would give me the peace that surpasses all understanding and the assurance of Your constant presence. Help me to wake with a renewed sense of trust in Your plan and a joyful anticipation of the good things You have in store. In Jesus' name, Amen.

## Prayers for Destiny Redemption
*Morning Prayers*

1. Gracious Lord, I come before You today, acknowledging that You are the author and perfecter of my faith and the one who holds my destiny in Your hands. I pray that You would redeem any past mistakes, failures, or detours and use them for Your glory and purpose. Help me to trust in Your redemptive power. In Jesus' name, Amen.

2. Loving Father, I thank You for the unique gifts, talents, and calling that You have placed within me. I pray that You would help me to discover and embrace the fullness of my destiny in You. Give me the courage to step out in faith and obedience, even when the path ahead is uncertain. In Jesus' name, Amen.

3. Mighty God, I pray for the breaking of any generational patterns, curses, or cycles of sin that may be hindering my destiny. I declare that I am a new creation in Christ and that my past and my family history do not define my future. Help me to walk in the freedom and victory that is mine through Your Son. In Jesus' name, Amen.

4. Compassionate God, I lift up any areas of my life where I have experienced disappointment, setbacks, or unfulfilled dreams. I pray that You would redeem these situations and use them as stepping stones towards the greater purposes You have for me. Help me to trust in Your timing and Your goodness. In Jesus' name,

Amen.

5. Gracious Lord, I pray for divine connections and relationships that will support and encourage me in the pursuit of my God-given destiny. Bring mentors, friends, and partners into my life who will speak truth, offer wisdom, and help me to grow in my faith and calling. In Jesus' name, Amen.

6. Loving Father, I ask for Your wisdom and discernment as I make decisions and navigate the choices that impact my destiny. Help me to seek Your will above all else and to be attentive to Your voice and leading. Give me the strength to obey Your guidance, even when it may be difficult or unpopular. In Jesus' name, Amen.

7. Mighty God, I pray for opportunities to use my gifts and passions to make a difference in the world and to advance Your Kingdom. Open doors for me to serve, lead, and influence others for Your glory. Help me to be a faithful steward of the destiny You have entrusted to me. In Jesus' name, Amen.

8. Compassionate God, I lift up any areas of my life where I have experienced pain, trauma, or brokenness. I pray that You would bring healing, restoration, and redemption to these places and use them as a testimony of Your grace and power. Help me to find purpose in my struggles and to use them to encourage others. In Jesus' name, Amen.

9. Gracious Lord, I pray for the strength and perseverance to overcome any obstacles, challenges, or opposition that may arise as I pursue my destiny. Remind me that greater is He that is in me than he that is in the world and that I can do all things through Christ who strengthens me. Help me to fix my eyes on You. In Jesus' name, Amen.

10. Loving Father, I thank You for the promise that You

have plans to prosper me and not to harm me, plans to give me hope and a future. I trust in Your love and Your desire to see me fulfil my God-given destiny. Help me to walk in obedience and faith, knowing that You are guiding my every step. In Jesus' name, Amen.

*Evening Prayers*

1. Gracious Lord, as I come to the end of this day, I thank You for Your faithfulness and the assurance that You are working all things together for my good and for Your glory. I surrender my plans, dreams, and desires into Your hands, trusting that Your purposes for me are perfect and good. In Jesus' name, Amen.

2. Loving Father, I confess any areas of my life where I have been striving in my own strength or seeking my own selfish ambitions. I pray that You would purify my heart and align my desires with Your will. Help me to find my identity and worth in You alone and to pursue my destiny with humility and grace. In Jesus' name, Amen.

3. Mighty God, I pray for the courage and boldness to live out my destiny, even in the face of fear, doubt, or opposition. Help me to trust in Your protection and provision and to stand firm in my faith. Give me the wisdom to discern Your voice and the strength to follow Your leading, no matter the cost. In Jesus' name, Amen.

4. Compassionate God, I lift up any relationships or connections that may be holding me back from embracing my God-given destiny. I pray that You would give me the discernment to know when to let go and the grace to do so with love and forgiveness. Surround me with people who will encourage and support me in my pursuit of Your will. In Jesus' name, Amen.

5. Gracious Lord, I thank You for the gift of redemption and the power of Your transforming love. I pray that You would continue to mold me into the person You have created me to be, refining my character and shaping my heart to reflect Your own. Help me to embrace the process of growth and sanctification as I journey towards my destiny. In Jesus' name, Amen.

6. Loving Father, I pray for the grace to trust in Your timing and to find contentment in each season of my life. Help me to embrace the unique opportunities and lessons that each chapter brings, knowing that You are using all things to prepare me for the fulfillment of my destiny. Give me a heart of gratitude and joy. In Jesus' name, Amen.

7. Mighty God, I pray for divine favor and open doors as I pursue the calling You have placed on my life. Remove any obstacles or hindrances that may stand in the way and make clear the path You have set before me. Help me to walk in obedience and faith, trusting in Your guidance and provision every step of the way. In Jesus' name, Amen.

8. Compassionate God, I lift up any areas of brokenness or woundedness in my life that may be hindering my ability to fully embrace my destiny. I pray for Your healing touch and the power of Your redemptive love to restore and transform me from the inside out. Use my testimony to bring hope and healing to others. In Jesus' name, Amen.

9. Gracious Lord, I thank You for the promise that You will complete the good work You have begun in me and that Your plans for me are filled with hope and a future. I trust in Your faithfulness and Your ability to bring all things to fruition in Your perfect timing. Help me to rest in Your love and to find my peace in You. In

Jesus' name, Amen.

10. Loving Father, as I lay down to sleep, I entrust my life, my future, and my destiny into Your loving hands. I pray that You would give me the peace that surpasses all understanding and the assurance of Your constant presence. Help me to wake with a renewed sense of purpose and excitement for the good things You have in store. In Jesus' name, Amen.

# CHAPTER 7: BATHSHEBA - FROM SCANDAL TO ROYALTY

## INTRODUCTION

The story of Bathsheba, found in the Bible in 2 Samuel 11-12 and 1 Kings 1-2, is a complex narrative of sin, redemption, and God's sovereign plan. Bathsheba, the wife of Uriah the Hittite, becomes involved in a scandalous affair with King David, which leads to a series of tragic events. However, God's grace and mercy are evident in Bathsheba's life, as He transforms her story from one of scandal to one of royalty.

In this chapter, we will explore the key events of Bathsheba's life, from her initial encounter with David to her role as the mother of King Solomon. We will examine the consequences of David's sin and the way in which God's justice and mercy are displayed in the lives of those involved.

As we delve into Bathsheba's story, we will also uncover valuable lessons about repentance, forgiveness, and the far-reaching impact of our choices. We will see how God can redeem even the most painful and shameful experiences for His glory and purposes.

The chapter will be structured as follows:

1. The Setting of Bathsheba's Story

2. David and Bathsheba's Scandalous Affair
3. The Consequences of David's Sin
4. Nathan's Confrontation and David's Repentance
5. The Death of David and Bathsheba's First Child
6. The Birth of Solomon and Bathsheba's Place in the Lineage of Christ
7. Bathsheba's Role in Securing Solomon's Throne
8. Lessons from Bathsheba's Life for Us Today

Following these sections, we will provide a series of heartfelt prayers inspired by Bathsheba's story. These prayers will be divided into two categories:

a. Prayers for mercy

b. Prayers to be exalted

Each prayer section will include ten prayer points, providing a total of 20 targeted prayers. These prayers will serve as a source of comfort, encouragement, and hope for those who, like Bathsheba, have experienced the pain of sin and the need for God's mercy and redemption.

Through this chapter, may we be reminded of the depth of God's love and the power of His transformative grace. May we find hope in the knowledge that no matter our past failings or the challenges we face, God can redeem our stories and use us for His glory.

**The Setting of Bathsheba's Story**

Bathsheba's story unfolds during the reign of King David, one of Israel's most renowned and beloved leaders. David, who had been chosen by God to lead His people, had experienced numerous victories and blessings throughout his life. However, as his power and influence grew, so did his vulnerability to temptation.

The story begins in Jerusalem, where David remains while his army is out fighting against the Ammonites. It was customary for kings to lead their armies into battle, but on this occasion, David stays behind, setting the stage for the events that would follow.

In those days, kings held absolute authority and their word was law. They had the power to make decisions that affected the lives of their subjects, and their actions were often beyond question or reproach.

It is against this backdrop that we encounter Bathsheba, the wife of Uriah the Hittite, one of David's loyal soldiers. Bathsheba's story takes place at a time when David's power and influence were at their peak, and his decisions, whether just or unjust, had far-reaching consequences for those under his rule.

It is important to recognize that in this context, Bathsheba was a victim of David's abuse of power, rather than an accomplice in his sin. As a woman in a patriarchal society, she had no legal recourse or means of refusing the king's advances. Her position was one of vulnerability and powerlessness, and she found herself caught in the web of David's wrongdoing.

The story of David and Bathsheba is a clear example of how power can be misused and how even the most respected leaders can fall into sin when they fail to exercise self-control and integrity. It also highlights the devastating impact that the actions of those in authority can have on the lives of the people they are meant to serve and protect.

As the narrative unfolds, we see how David's sin with Bathsheba sets in motion a series of tragic events that would have profound consequences for his reign and his family. Despite Bathsheba's innocence in the matter, she finds herself caught up in the drama and heartache that result from David's moral failure.

The setting of Bathsheba's story serves as a poignant reminder of the importance of character, integrity, and the proper use of power and authority. It also underscores the need for those in positions of influence to be accountable for their actions and to exercise their leadership with wisdom, compassion, and a deep respect for the well-being of those they serve.

## David and Bathsheba's Scandalous Affair

One evening, while walking on the roof of his palace, David catches sight of Bathsheba bathing. The Bible describes her as "very beautiful" (2 Samuel 11:2). Despite knowing that Bathsheba is married, David sends for her and sleeps with her. As the king, David's actions would have been seen as an exercise of his authority, and Bathsheba, as his subject, would have had little choice but to comply with his demands. As a result, Bathsheba becomes pregnant.

In an attempt to cover up his sin, David summons Uriah back from the battlefield, hoping that he will sleep with his wife and believe the child to be his own. However, Uriah, being a man of honor, refuses to enjoy the comforts of home while his fellow soldiers are still fighting. Frustrated by this turn of events, David sends Uriah back to the front lines, carrying his own death warrant. David instructs Joab, his commander, to place Uriah in the fiercest part of the battle and then withdraw, ensuring Uriah's death.

## The Consequences of David's Sin

After Uriah's death, David takes Bathsheba as his wife, believing that his sin has been concealed. However, the Bible states that "the thing David had done displeased the Lord" (2 Samuel 11:27). God sends the prophet Nathan to confront David, using a parable to expose the king's guilt.

David, upon realizing the gravity of his sin, confesses and repents before God. While God forgives David, He also makes it clear that there will be consequences for his actions. The child conceived by David and Bathsheba falls ill, and despite David's fervent prayers and fasting, the child dies.

This tragedy marks a turning point in David's life and reign. The once-mighty king is humbled, and his family begins to experience the effects of his sin, as prophesied by Nathan.

## Nathan's Confrontation and David's Repentance

The prophet Nathan's confrontation of David stands as a pivotal moment in the narrative. Nathan presents a parable to the king, telling of a rich man who takes a poor man's beloved lamb to feed a visitor, despite having many lambs of his own. David, enraged by the story, declares that the rich man deserves to die for his actions.

At this point, Nathan boldly declares, "You are the man!" (2 Samuel 12:7). He exposes David's sin and the way in which he had abused his power and position. Nathan also reveals the consequences that will follow, including strife within David's own household.

Faced with the weight of his sin, David responds with deep repentance. He acknowledges his transgressions and seeks God's mercy and forgiveness. David's prayer of repentance, recorded in Psalm 51, stands as a powerful example of contrition and the desire for restoration.

## The Death of David and Bathsheba's First Child

Despite David's repentance, the consequences of his sin begin to unfold. The child conceived by David and Bathsheba becomes ill, and David pleads with God for the child's life. He fasts, prays, and spends nights lying on the ground, hoping for God's mercy.

However, on the seventh day, the child dies. David's servants, fearing his reaction, are reluctant to tell him. When David realizes what has happened, he rises, washes himself, and goes to the house of the Lord to worship. He demonstrates acceptance of God's judgment and finds comfort in the knowledge that he will one day be reunited with his child.

This tragic event serves as a reminder of the far-reaching consequences of sin and the importance of obedience and righteousness before God.

## The Birth of Solomon and Bathsheba's Place in the Lineage of

**Christ**

After the death of their first child, David comforts Bathsheba, and she conceives again. This time, she gives birth to a son named Solomon, whose name means "peace." The Bible states that "the Lord loved him" and sends word through Nathan that Solomon should also be called Jedidiah, meaning "beloved of the Lord" (2 Samuel 12:24-25).

Solomon goes on to succeed David as king of Israel and is known for his wisdom, wealth, and the construction of the first Temple in Jerusalem. Bathsheba, as the mother of Solomon, secures a place of honor and influence in the royal court.

Remarkably, despite the scandalous nature of her relationship with David, Bathsheba is included in the lineage of Jesus Christ. In Matthew 1:6, she is referred to as "the wife of Uriah," emphasizing God's grace and His ability to redeem even the most complicated and painful situations.

**Bathsheba's Role in Securing Solomon's Throne**

In 1 Kings 1, as David nears the end of his life, his son Adonijah attempts to claim the throne for himself. Bathsheba, along with the prophet Nathan, acts decisively to ensure that Solomon, the rightful heir, becomes king.

Bathsheba goes to David and reminds him of his promise that Solomon would reign after him. She also informs him of Adonijah's actions and the potential threat to Solomon's succession. David, in response, instructs that Solomon be anointed and proclaimed as king, thus securing his place on the throne.

Bathsheba's actions demonstrate her wisdom, courage, and commitment to God's plan. Despite her past, she becomes an instrumental figure in the establishment of Solomon's reign and the continuation of the Davidic dynasty.

**Lessons from Bathsheba's Life for Us Today**

Bathsheba's story offers valuable lessons and insights for our lives today:

1. Sin has consequences: David and Bathsheba's sin had far-reaching effects on their lives and the lives of those around them. This serves as a reminder that our actions, both good and bad, have consequences and can impact others in significant ways.

2. Repentance and forgiveness are possible: Despite the gravity of David's sin, he found forgiveness and restoration through sincere repentance. This demonstrates that no matter how far we may have strayed, God's mercy and grace are available to those who seek Him with a contrite heart.

3. God can redeem painful situations: Bathsheba's story, marked by scandal and tragedy, is ultimately redeemed by God's sovereign plan. Her inclusion in the lineage of Christ serves as a powerful reminder that God can bring beauty from ashes and use even the most difficult circumstances for His glory.

4. Our past does not define our future: Bathsheba's life demonstrates that our past mistakes and the sins committed against us do not have to determine the course of our lives. Through God's grace, we can be transformed and used for His purposes, regardless of our background or experiences.

5. Wisdom and courage are essential: Bathsheba's actions in securing Solomon's throne showcase the importance of wisdom and courage in navigating difficult situations. As believers, we are called to seek God's wisdom and act with boldness in the face of challenges and opposition.

As we reflect on Bathsheba's story, may we be encouraged by the depth of God's love and the transformative power of His grace. May we find hope in the knowledge that no matter our past or present circumstances, God can redeem our stories and use us for His glory.

## **Prayers for Mercy**

1. Heavenly Father, I come before You today with a humble and contrite heart, acknowledging my need for Your mercy. Like David, I have sinned and fallen short of Your glory. I ask for Your forgiveness and the cleansing power of Your grace to wash over me. In Jesus' name, Amen.

2. Merciful God, I confess that there are times when I have chosen my own desires over Your will, just as David did with Bathsheba. I pray that You would convict me of my sin and lead me to true repentance. Help me to turn away from temptation and to seek Your face above all else. In Jesus' name, Amen.

3. Gracious Lord, I thank You for the example of David's repentance and the assurance of Your mercy and forgiveness. I pray that You would give me a heart that is quick to acknowledge my failings and to seek Your mercy. May I never take Your grace for granted, but instead live each day in humble gratitude for Your love. In Jesus' name, Amen.

4. Compassionate Father, I bring before You the consequences of my sin and the pain that I have caused others. I ask for Your mercy and healing for those who have been hurt by my actions. I pray that You would restore what has been broken and bring reconciliation and peace. In Jesus' name, Amen.

5. Loving God, I praise You for Your unfailing mercy and the way in which You pursue us even in our darkest moments. I pray that I would never run from Your presence, but instead, like David, run towards You in my time of need. Thank You for Your open arms and Your willingness to forgive. In Jesus' name, Amen.

6. Merciful Savior, I come before You today, recognizing my need for Your mercy in every area of my life. I pray that You would search my heart and reveal any hidden sins or areas of rebellion. Give me the courage to confess and the strength to turn away from anything that hinders my relationship with You. In Jesus' name, Amen.

7. Gracious Redeemer, I thank You for the power of Your mercy to transform lives and to bring beauty from ashes. I pray that You would use my story, like Bathsheba's, to display Your grace and to bring hope to others who are struggling with sin and shame. May my life be a testament to Your redeeming love. In Jesus' name, Amen.

8. Compassionate Father, I lift up to You those who are suffering under the weight of their sin and the consequences of their actions. I pray that You would surround them with Your mercy and love, and that they would find hope and healing in Your presence. Give them the courage to seek Your forgiveness and the strength to walk in newness of life. In Jesus' name, Amen.

9. Merciful God, I praise You for Your patience and long-suffering towards us, even when we stumble and fall. I pray that I would never take Your mercy for granted, but instead live each day in reverence and awe of Your grace. Help me to extend that same mercy and forgiveness to others, just as You have extended it to me. In Jesus' name, Amen.

10. Loving Lord, I thank You for the assurance that Your mercy is new every morning and that Your love never fails. I pray that I would wake each day with a heart that is eager to receive Your mercy and to walk in Your ways. May my life be a living testimony of Your grace

and the transformative power of Your love. In Jesus' name, Amen.

## **Prayers to Be Exalted**

1. Gracious Father, I come before You today with a heart that desires to be exalted in Your presence. I pray that You would lift me up from the depths of my sin and shame and set my feet upon the solid rock of Your love. Help me to trust in Your plan to transform my story for Your glory. In Jesus' name, Amen.

2. Sovereign God, I acknowledge that true exaltation comes not from the praise of men, but from a life that is surrendered to Your will. I pray that You would give me a heart that seeks Your face above all else and that delights in Your presence. May my life be a living sacrifice, holy and pleasing to You. In Jesus' name, Amen.

3. Merciful Lord, I thank You for the example of Bathsheba, whose story demonstrates Your ability to exalt those who have been humbled by sin and circumstances. I pray that You would do the same in my life, lifting me up from the ashes of my past and giving me a new identity in Christ. In Jesus' name, Amen.

4. Gracious Redeemer, I pray that You would use the trials and challenges of my life to refine my character and to prepare me for the plans You have for me. Help me to trust in Your timing and Your methods, knowing that You are working all things together for my good and Your glory. In Jesus' name, Amen.

5. Loving Father, I praise You for Your faithfulness and Your commitment to fulfilling Your purposes in my life. I pray that You would give me the patience and perseverance to wait upon Your timing for exaltation, trusting that You will lift me up in due season. May I

find my joy and satisfaction in Your presence alone. In Jesus' name, Amen.

6. Sovereign God, I surrender my desires for recognition and success into Your hands, acknowledging that true exaltation comes from a life that is aligned with Your will. I pray that You would give me a heart that is humble and submitted to Your leadership, and that seeks to glorify You in all things. In Jesus' name, Amen.

7. Merciful Lord, I thank You for the promise that those who humble themselves before You will be exalted in due time. I pray that You would cultivate in me a spirit of humility and servanthood, and that I would trust in Your plan to promote and prosper me according to Your perfect will. In Jesus' name, Amen.

8. Gracious Redeemer, I pray that You would use my story of transformation and exaltation to bring hope and encouragement to others who are struggling. Help me to be a light in the darkness and a testament to Your redeeming power. May my life point others to the hope and healing that can be found in You alone. In Jesus' name, Amen.

9. Loving Father, I praise You for Your wisdom and Your understanding that surpasses all human knowledge. I pray that You would give me the discernment to navigate the challenges and opportunities of life, and to make choices that honor You and align with Your plans for my exaltation. May I trust in Your guidance and lean not on my own understanding. In Jesus' name, Amen.

10. Sovereign God, I thank You for the assurance that my exaltation and success are ultimately in Your hands. I pray that I would rest in Your love and Your provision, knowing that You are working behind the scenes to bring about Your purposes in my life. May I live each

day in joyful anticipation of the good things You have in store for me, both in this life and in the life to come. In Jesus' name, Amen.

# CHAPTER 8: MARY - A LIFE SURRENDERED TO GOD'S WILL

## INTRODUCTION

The story of Mary, the mother of Jesus, is a remarkable example of faith, obedience, and surrender to the will of God. Throughout her life, Mary consistently demonstrated a heart that was wholly devoted to her Heavenly Father, even in the face of unexpected challenges and seemingly impossible circumstances.

In this chapter, we will explore the key aspects of Mary's life that showcase her unwavering commitment to God's plan. We will examine her response to the angel Gabriel's announcement of her miraculous conception, her trust in God's ability to perform the impossible, and her willingness to embrace the unique calling placed upon her life.

As we delve into Mary's story, we will also highlight the significance of her words at the wedding feast in Cana, where she instructed the servants to follow Jesus' commands. This incident reveals Mary's deep understanding of her son's divine nature and her desire for others to align their lives with His will.

Furthermore, we will consider Mary's unwavering devotion to Jesus, even in the midst of the pain and suffering she witnessed during His crucifixion. Her presence at the foot of the cross serves as a powerful testament to her love, strength, and resilience in the face of unimaginable grief.

Throughout this chapter, we will draw valuable lessons and insights from Mary's life that are particularly relevant for modern women. We will explore the importance of aligning our lives with God's will, cultivating a strong faith that believes in the impossible, pursuing the Great Commission with passion and fervency, and walking in wisdom to leave a lasting, eternal legacy.

The chapter will be structured as follows:

1. Mary's Encounter with the Angel Gabriel
2. The Miraculous Conception: A Testament to Mary's Faith
3. Mary's Song of Praise: The Magnificat
4. Jesus' First Miracle at Cana: Mary's Instructions to the Servants
5. Mary at the Foot of the Cross: A Mother's Love and Devotion
6. Lessons from Mary's Life for Modern Women
7. The Importance of Aligning with God's Will
8. Cultivating a Faith That Believes in the Impossible
9. Pursuing the Great Commission with Fervency
10. Walking in Wisdom to Obtain an Eternal Legacy

Following these sections, we will provide a series of heartfelt prayers inspired by Mary's life and example. These prayers will be divided into four categories, each focusing on a specific aspect of Mary's faith and journey:

a. Prayers to always align with God's will

b. Prayers for miracle conception

c. Prayers for wisdom, honor, and an eternal legacy

d. Prayers to expand the kingdom of God and pursue the Great Commission with fervency

Each prayer section will include ten prayer points for both morning and evening, providing a total of 80 targeted prayers. These prayers will serve as a powerful resource for women seeking to emulate Mary's faith, obedience, and devotion to God in their own lives.

As we embark on this exploration of Mary's life and the lessons she offers, may we be inspired to cultivate a deeper trust in God, a willingness to embrace His plans for our lives, and a passionate commitment to furthering His kingdom here on earth. May Mary's example of faith, wisdom, and surrender encourage us to leave a lasting legacy that brings glory and honor to our Heavenly Father.

**Mary's Encounter with the Angel Gabriel**

The story of Mary begins with a remarkable encounter with the angel Gabriel, as recorded in Luke 1:26-38. Gabriel appears to Mary, a young virgin betrothed to a man named Joseph, and greets her with the words, "Rejoice, highly favored one, the Lord is with you; blessed are you among women!" (Luke 1:28).

Mary is initially troubled by this greeting, but Gabriel reassures her, explaining that she has found favor with God. He then reveals the astonishing news that Mary will conceive and give birth to a son, who will be named Jesus and will be called the Son of the Highest. Gabriel declares that Jesus will reign over the house of Jacob forever and that His kingdom will have no end.

Mary, perplexed by this announcement, asks, "How can this be, since I do not know a man?" (Luke 1:34). Gabriel explains that the Holy Spirit will come upon her and that the power of the Highest will overshadow her, making the child she will bear the Son of God.

In a remarkable display of faith and submission, Mary responds, "Behold the maidservant of the Lord! Let it be to me according to your word" (Luke 1:38). Her willingness to embrace God's plan, even in the face of uncertainty and potential social stigma, sets the stage for the miraculous events that will follow.

### The Miraculous Conception: A Testament to Mary's Faith

As the angel Gabriel declared, Mary's conception of Jesus is a miraculous work of the Holy Spirit. This event is a powerful testament to Mary's faith and her willingness to trust in God's plan, even when it defied natural understanding.

The virgin birth of Jesus is a cornerstone of Christian theology, affirming His divine nature and His unique role as the Savior of the world. Mary's faith and obedience in accepting this miracle as a fulfillment of God's promise demonstrate her deep trust in God and her surrender to His purposes.

Throughout the Gospels, we see evidence of Mary's continued faith and devotion to God. She ponders the events of Jesus' life in her heart (Luke 2:19, 51), seeks to understand His mission and teachings (Luke 2:48-50), and remains a faithful follower even in the face of the pain and sorrow of the crucifixion (John 19:25-27).

Mary's miraculous conception and her unwavering faith serve as an inspiration and example for believers today, encouraging us to trust in God's power and to embrace His plans for our lives, even when they may seem impossible or challenging from a human perspective.

### Mary's Song of Praise: The Magnificat

After her encounter with the angel Gabriel and her visit to her relative Elizabeth, Mary gives voice to her joy and praise in a beautiful song known as the Magnificat (Luke 1:46-55). This song, which has become a beloved part of Christian worship and liturgy, reveals the depth of Mary's faith and her understanding of God's character and purposes.

In the Magnificat, Mary declares,

"My soul magnifies the Lord,

And my spirit has rejoiced in God my Savior.

For He has regarded the lowly state of His maidservant;

For behold, henceforth all generations will call me blessed.

For He who is mighty has done great things for me,

And holy is His name.

And His mercy is on those who fear Him

From generation to generation.

He has shown strength with His arm;

He has scattered the proud in the imagination of their hearts.

He has put down the mighty from their thrones,

And exalted the lowly.

He has filled the hungry with good things,

And the rich He has sent away empty.

He has helped His servant Israel,

In remembrance of His mercy,

As He spoke to our fathers,

To Abraham and to his seed forever."

Mary recognizes the great things that God has done for her and acknowledges her humble status as His servant. Mary's song also highlights God's mercy, His faithfulness to His promises, and His concern for the lowly and oppressed. She proclaims, "He has shown strength with His arm; He has scattered the proud in the imagination of their hearts. He has put down the mighty from their thrones, and exalted the lowly. He has filled the hungry with good things, and the rich He has sent away empty" (Luke 1:51-53).

These words reveal Mary's understanding of God as a God of justice and compassion, who uplifts the humble and brings down the proud. Her song foreshadows the teachings and ministry of Jesus, who will declare good news to the poor, liberty to the captives, and the year of the Lord's favor (Luke 4:18-19).

The Magnificat serves as a powerful reminder of God's

faithfulness and the transformative power of His love and grace. It encourages believers to join Mary in magnifying the Lord and rejoicing in His goodness, even in the midst of life's challenges and uncertainties.

**Jesus' First Miracle at Cana: Mary's Instructions to the Servants**

The Gospel of John records Jesus' first miracle, which took place at a wedding feast in Cana of Galilee (John 2:1-11). Mary, who was present at the wedding, plays a significant role in this event, demonstrating her faith in Jesus and her desire for others to follow His instructions.

When the wine runs out at the wedding feast, Mary approaches Jesus and informs Him of the situation. Jesus initially responds, "Woman, what does your concern have to do with Me? My hour has not yet come" (John 2:4). However, Mary is not deterred by this response. Instead, she turns to the servants and instructs them, "Whatever He says to you, do it" (John 2:5).

Mary's words reveal her confidence in Jesus' power and authority, as well as her willingness to trust in His timing and methods. She demonstrates a deep understanding of Jesus' identity and mission, even before He has begun His public ministry.

As a result of Mary's faith and Jesus' miraculous intervention, the water in the stone jars is transformed into the finest wine, revealing Jesus' glory and leading His disciples to believe in Him (John 2:11).

Mary's instructions to the servants at the wedding feast serve as a powerful reminder for believers today. We are called to trust in Jesus' words and to obey His commands, even when they may not align with our own understanding or expectations. As we follow Mary's example of faith and obedience, we open ourselves to experiencing the transformative power of Christ in our lives and in the lives of those around us.

## Mary at the Foot of the Cross: A Mother's Love and Devotion

One of the most poignant moments in Mary's life is her presence at the foot of the cross during Jesus' crucifixion. The Gospel of John records this scene, highlighting Mary's deep love for her son and her unwavering devotion to Him, even in the face of unimaginable sorrow and pain.

As Jesus hangs on the cross, He sees His mother and the disciple whom He loved standing nearby. In a tender moment of care and provision, Jesus entrusts Mary to the beloved disciple, saying, "Woman, behold your son!" and to the disciple, "Behold your mother!" (John 19:26-27). From that hour, the disciple took Mary into his own home, fulfilling Jesus' desire for her to be cared for and supported.

Mary's presence at the crucifixion is a testament to her strength, courage, and resilience. Despite the agony of watching her son suffer and die, she remains steadfast in her love and commitment to Him. Her presence also serves as a reminder of the prophecy spoken by Simeon when Jesus was presented at the temple as an infant: "A sword will pierce through your own soul also" (Luke 2:35).

Mary's experience at the foot of the cross has made her a powerful symbol of comfort and empathy for those who suffer. Her ability to endure the deepest of sorrows and to find hope and purpose in the midst of tragedy serves as an inspiration for believers facing their own trials and challenges.

Moreover, Mary's presence at the crucifixion highlights the significance of faithful endurance and the importance of standing with others in their moments of pain and suffering. As we seek to follow Christ and to live out His love in the world, we are called to bear one another's burdens and to offer hope, compassion, and support to those who are hurting.

## Lessons from Mary's Life for Modern Women

Mary's life and example offer valuable lessons and insights for women today, particularly in the areas of faith, obedience, and devotion to God. Here are a few key takeaways:

1. Embracing God's will: Mary's response to the angel Gabriel, "Let it be to me according to your word" (Luke 1:38), demonstrates the importance of surrendering our lives to God's plan and purpose. As women, we are called to trust in God's wisdom and to follow His leading, even when it may require stepping out in faith or facing challenges.

2. Cultivating a heart of worship: Mary's song of praise, the Magnificat, reveals the importance of cultivating a heart of worship and gratitude. By focusing on God's goodness and faithfulness, we can find joy and strength, even in the midst of life's uncertainties and trials.

3. Trusting in Jesus' power and authority: Mary's instructions to the servants at the wedding feast in Cana, "Whatever He says to you, do it" (John 2:5), emphasize the importance of trusting in Jesus' words and obeying His commands. As we follow Mary's example of faith and obedience, we open ourselves to experiencing the transformative power of Christ in our lives.

4. Persevering in love and devotion: Mary's presence at the foot of the cross highlights the significance of faithful endurance and the importance of standing with others in their moments of pain and suffering. As women, we are called to bear one another's burdens and to offer hope, compassion, and support to those who are hurting.

5. Leaving a lasting legacy: Mary's life and legacy have had a profound impact on the Church and on countless believers throughout history. Her example encourages us to live our lives in a way that points others to Christ

and leaves a lasting impact for His kingdom.

As modern women seeking to follow Christ and to make a difference in the world, we can draw strength and inspiration from Mary's example. By embracing God's will, cultivating a heart of worship, trusting in Jesus' power, persevering in love, and seeking to leave a lasting legacy, we can become women of faith, purpose, and impact, just as Mary was.

**The Importance of Aligning with God's Will**

One of the central themes of Mary's life is the importance of aligning our lives with God's will and purposes. From the moment of the angel Gabriel's announcement to her final moments at the foot of the cross, Mary consistently demonstrated a heart of submission and obedience to God's plan.

Mary's response to Gabriel's message, "Let it be to me according to your word" (Luke 1:38), sets the tone for her entire life and ministry. Despite the challenges and uncertainties that lay ahead, Mary chose to trust in God's wisdom and to surrender her own plans and desires to His perfect will.

This willingness to align with God's purposes is a crucial lesson for believers today. In a world that often encourages us to pursue our own goals and ambitions, Mary's example reminds us that true fulfillment and purpose are found in submitting our lives to God and seeking His will above all else.

Aligning with God's will requires a posture of humility, trust, and obedience. It means recognizing that God's ways are higher than our ways and that His plans are ultimately for our good and His glory. It involves a willingness to step out in faith, even when the path ahead may be unclear or challenging.

As we seek to follow Mary's example of alignment with God's will, we can find comfort and strength in the knowledge that God is faithful and that His purposes will prevail. By surrendering our lives to Him and trusting in His guidance, we open ourselves to experiencing the fullness of His blessings and the joy of participating in His redemptive work in the world.

**Cultivating a Faith That Believes in the Impossible**

Another powerful lesson from Mary's life is the importance of cultivating a faith that believes in the impossible. Throughout her story, Mary demonstrated a deep trust in God's power and a willingness to embrace His miraculous work in her life.

When the angel Gabriel announced that Mary would conceive and give birth to the Son of God, she was faced with a situation that defied natural understanding. Yet, rather than responding with doubt or disbelief, Mary declared, "Let it be to me according to your word" (Luke 1:38). Her faith in God's power and His ability to do the impossible was a defining characteristic of her life and ministry.

Mary's faith was not a blind or naive trust, but rather a deep conviction rooted in her knowledge of God's character and His faithfulness to His promises. Her song of praise, the Magnificat, reveals a profound understanding of God's mercy, strength, and concern for the lowly and oppressed.

Cultivating a faith like Mary's involves nurturing a relationship with God through prayer, worship, and the study of His Word. It means fixing our eyes on Jesus, the author and perfecter of our faith, and trusting in His power to do exceedingly abundantly above all that we could ask or imagine.

As we seek to follow Mary's example of faith, we can find encouragement in the knowledge that nothing is impossible with God. Whether we are facing personal challenges, seemingly insurmountable obstacles, or opportunities to participate in God's miraculous work in the world, we can trust in His power and faithfulness to bring about His purposes.

By cultivating a faith that believes in the impossible, we position ourselves to experience the fullness of God's blessings and to be used by Him in powerful and transformative ways. Like Mary, we can become vessels of His grace and love, bearing witness to His glory and inviting others to put their trust in Him.

**Pursuing the Great Commission with Fervency**

While Mary is not typically associated with the Great Commission in the same way as the apostles or other early church leaders, her life and example nonetheless offer valuable insights for believers seeking to pursue God's call to make disciples of all nations.

Throughout the Gospels, we see Mary's unwavering devotion to Jesus and her support of His ministry. From her presence at the wedding feast in Cana, where she encouraged the servants to follow Jesus' instructions, to her faithful vigil at the foot of the cross, Mary consistently demonstrated a heart for God's purposes and a desire to see others come to faith in Christ.

Moreover, Mary's own journey of faith and obedience serves as a powerful witness to the transformative power of the gospel. Her willingness to surrender her life to God's plan and to trust in His miraculous work in her life speaks to the hope and salvation that are available to all who put their faith in Christ.

As believers seeking to pursue the Great Commission with fervency, we can draw inspiration from Mary's example of devotion, faith, and witness. We are called to be ambassadors for Christ, proclaiming the good news of His love and salvation to a world in need.

Pursuing the Great Commission with fervency involves a commitment to prayer, a willingness to step out in faith, and a heart for the lost and hurting. It means being attentive to the opportunities God places before us to share His love and truth with others, whether in our own communities or in the uttermost parts of the earth.

Like Mary, we may face challenges, uncertainties, and even opposition as we seek to follow God's call to make disciples. Yet, we can find strength and courage in the knowledge that God is with us and that His purposes will prevail. By fixing our eyes on Jesus and surrendering our lives to His will, we can become effective and passionate advocates for His kingdom, inviting others to experience the transformative power of His grace and love.

**Walking in Wisdom to Obtain an Eternal Legacy**

Finally, Mary's life and legacy offer valuable insights for believers seeking to walk in wisdom and to leave a lasting impact for God's kingdom. Throughout her story, Mary demonstrated a heart of wisdom and understanding, rooted in her deep relationship with God and her attentiveness to His will and purposes.

The Gospels record several instances where Mary pondered the events of Jesus' life and ministry in her heart (Luke 2:19, 51), seeking to understand their significance and to align her own life with God's unfolding plan. Her song of praise, the Magnificat, reveals a profound understanding of God's character and His work in the world, as well as a heart of humility and surrender.

As believers seeking to walk in wisdom and to obtain an eternal legacy, we can learn from Mary's example of reflection, obedience, and devotion. Walking in wisdom involves seeking God's guidance and direction in every area of our lives, and being attentive to His still, small voice as He leads and directs our steps.

It also involves a commitment to living our lives in a way that honors God and reflects His character and purposes. Like Mary, we are called to be vessels of His grace and love, bearing witness to the hope and salvation that are found in Christ alone.

Obtaining an eternal legacy means investing our time, talents, and resources in things that have lasting value and significance. It means seeking first God's kingdom and His righteousness, and trusting that He will use our lives to accomplish His purposes and to bring glory to His name.

As we follow Mary's example of wisdom and devotion, we can find encouragement in the knowledge that our lives and legacies are secure in Christ. By walking in obedience to His will and seeking to honor Him in all that we do, we can leave a lasting impact for His kingdom that will endure long after we are gone.

Ultimately, Mary's life and legacy stand as a powerful testimony to the transformative power of God's grace and the incredible ways in which He can use ordinary people to accomplish His extraordinary purposes. As we seek to follow in her footsteps, may we find the courage, wisdom, and faith to surrender our lives to Him and to trust in His power to bring about His perfect will in and through us.

## Prayers to Always Align with God's Will
*Morning Prayers*

1. Heavenly Father, as I begin this day, I surrender my will to Yours. Like Mary, I desire to align my heart and mind with Your perfect plan for my life. Grant me the grace to trust in Your wisdom and to follow Your leading, even when the path ahead is unclear. In Jesus' name, Amen.

2. Lord Jesus, I acknowledge that Your ways are higher than my ways, and Your thoughts are higher than my thoughts. Help me to lay aside my own desires and preferences, and to embrace the unique calling and purpose You have ordained for me. May my life be a living testament to Your goodness and faithfulness. In Jesus' name, Amen.

3. Holy Spirit, I invite You to guide and direct my steps today. Help me to be attentive to Your still, small voice, and to respond with obedience and faith. When I am tempted to go my own way, remind me of Mary's example of surrender and trust. May my life be a reflection of Your love and grace. In Jesus' name, Amen.

4. Gracious God, I pray that You would align my priorities and values with Your heart. Help me to seek first Your kingdom and righteousness, and to trust that all other things will be added unto me. May I find my joy and satisfaction in pleasing You and bringing glory to Your name. In Jesus' name, Amen.

5. Loving Father, I surrender my plans and dreams into Your hands. Like Mary, I declare, "Behold, I am the servant of the Lord; let it be to me according to Your word." I trust that Your plans for me are good, and that You are working all things together for my ultimate benefit. In Jesus' name, Amen.

6. Merciful God, I confess that there are times when I struggle to submit to Your will. Help me to overcome my doubts, fears, and resistance, and to trust in Your loving kindness and faithfulness. Strengthen my resolve to follow You, even when the cost is high. In Jesus' name, Amen.

7. Sovereign Lord, I acknowledge that You are the Potter, and I am the clay. Mold me and shape me according to Your perfect design. Help me to yield to Your transforming work in my life, and to embrace the unique beauty and purpose You have created me for. In Jesus' name, Amen.

8. Gracious Father, I pray that You would give me a heart of discernment and wisdom to recognize Your will in every situation. Help me to seek godly counsel and to immerse myself in Your Word, so that I may know Your heart and walk in Your ways. In Jesus' name, Amen.

9. Loving God, I thank You for the gift of free will, and for the privilege of choosing to follow You. Help me to use this gift wisely, and to always choose the path of obedience and surrender. May my life be a living sacrifice, holy and pleasing in Your sight. In Jesus'

name, Amen.

10. Heavenly Father, I pray that You would use my life as a vessel for Your glory and purposes. Like Mary, I want to be a willing and obedient servant, ready to respond to Your call with faith and courage. May my life be a testament to the power of a surrendered heart. In Jesus' name, Amen.

*Evening Prayers*

1. Gracious God, as I come to the end of this day, I lay before You all the moments where I struggled to align my will with Yours. I ask for Your forgiveness and cleansing, and I pray that You would renew my mind and transform my heart to desire what You desire. In Jesus' name, Amen.

2. Loving Father, I thank You for the example of Mary, who trusted in Your plan even when it seemed impossible or costly. Help me to cultivate a heart of faith and obedience, and to trust that Your ways are always perfect, even when I cannot see the full picture. In Jesus' name, Amen.

3. Holy Spirit, I invite You to search my heart and reveal any areas where I am resisting or disobeying God's will. Give me the courage to confess and repent of any self-will or pride, and to submit myself fully to Your leading and guidance. In Jesus' name, Amen.

4. Sovereign Lord, I surrender to You all the worries, fears, and burdens I am carrying. I trust that You are in control, and that Your plans for me are good. Help me to rest in Your love and care, knowing that You are working all things together for my ultimate good and Your glory. In Jesus' name, Amen.

5. Merciful God, I confess that there are times when I struggle to discern Your will or to trust in Your timing.

Help me to lean on Your wisdom and understanding, and to wait patiently for Your perfect plan to unfold. Give me the strength to persevere in faith, even when the waiting is difficult. In Jesus' name, Amen.

6. Gracious Father, I pray that You would surround me with godly mentors and examples who can encourage and inspire me to walk in obedience and surrender. Help me to learn from the faith and testimony of others, and to be a source of encouragement and support to those around me. In Jesus' name, Amen.

7. Loving God, I thank You for the peace and joy that comes from aligning my life with Your will. Help me to find my deepest satisfaction and fulfillment in pleasing You and serving Your purposes. May my life be a fragrant offering, acceptable and pleasing in Your sight. In Jesus' name, Amen.

8. Holy Spirit, I ask that You would fill me afresh with Your presence and power. Give me the boldness and courage to obey God's will, even when it requires sacrifice or discomfort. Help me to trust in Your strength and provision, knowing that Your grace is sufficient for every task. In Jesus' name, Amen.

9. Sovereign Lord, I declare that Your will be done in my life, on earth as it is in heaven. I pray that Your kingdom would come and Your purposes be accomplished through me. Use me as a vessel of Your love, grace, and truth, and may my life bring glory and honor to Your name. In Jesus' name, Amen.

10. Heavenly Father, as I prepare to rest this night, I entrust my life and my future into Your loving hands. I pray that You would give me the grace to surrender to Your will afresh each day, and to walk in the path You have ordained for me. May I find my peace and security in Your unfailing love and faithfulness. In Jesus' name,

Amen.

## Prayers for Miracle Conception

*Morning Prayers*

1. Heavenly Father, I come before You today with a heart full of faith and expectation. I believe that, like Mary, I too can experience the miracle of conception by the power of Your Holy Spirit. I ask that You would open my womb and bless me with the gift of a child, according to Your perfect will and timing. In Jesus' name, Amen.

2. Gracious God, I thank You for the example of Mary, whose faith and obedience paved the way for the miraculous conception of our Savior. I pray that You would strengthen my own faith and help me to trust in Your ability to do the impossible in my life. May my heart be filled with the same joy and wonder that Mary experienced as she carried the Son of God in her womb. In Jesus' name, Amen.

3. Loving Father, I surrender my desires and plans for parenthood into Your hands. I trust that Your timing and Your ways are perfect, even when they differ from my own. Help me to wait patiently on You, knowing that You are able to bring forth life and fruitfulness in Your appointed season. In Jesus' name, Amen.

4. Holy Spirit, I invite You to overshadow me with Your presence and power, just as You did with Mary. I pray that You would create within me a clean heart and renew a right spirit within me, making me a vessel fit for the miraculous work You desire to do in my life. In Jesus' name, Amen.

5. Merciful God, I confess any fear, doubt, or unbelief that may be hindering my faith for a miracle conception. I choose to fix my eyes on You, the author and perfecter

of my faith, and to trust in Your unlimited power and goodness. Help me to stand firm on Your promises and to expect great things from Your hand. In Jesus' name, Amen.

6. Sovereign Lord, I declare Your Word over my life and my body. I believe that no word from You will ever fail, and that Your plans and purposes for me will be accomplished. I speak life and fruitfulness over my womb, and I trust that Your creative power is at work within me. In Jesus' name, Amen.

7. Gracious Father, I pray that You would surround me with a community of faith-filled believers who can stand with me in prayer and encouragement as I believe for a miracle conception. Help me to find strength and support in the Body of Christ, and to be a source of hope and inspiration to others who may be facing similar challenges. In Jesus' name, Amen.

8. Loving God, I thank You for the gift of motherhood and for the privilege of partnering with You in the creation of new life. I pray that You would prepare my heart and my home for the blessing of a child, and that You would use my story to bring glory and honor to Your name. In Jesus' name, Amen.

9. Holy Spirit, I ask that You would fill me with Your peace and joy as I wait upon the Lord for a miracle conception. Help me to find my contentment and satisfaction in Christ alone, and to trust that His grace is sufficient for me in every season of life. May my heart overflow with gratitude and praise for all that You have done and all that You have yet to do. In Jesus' name, Amen.

10. Heavenly Father, I come into agreement with Your will and Your Word concerning my life and my family. I declare that I am fearfully and wonderfully made, and

that my body is a temple of the Holy Spirit. I pray that You would align every cell, tissue, and organ with Your divine design, and that You would bring forth the miracle of life within me. In Jesus' name, Amen.

*Evening Prayers*

1. Gracious God, as I come to the end of this day, I lay before You all my hopes and dreams for a miracle conception. I trust that You are able to do exceedingly abundantly above all that I could ask or imagine, and I surrender my desires into Your loving hands. May Your will be done in my life and in my family. In Jesus' name, Amen.

2. Loving Father, I thank You for the gift of faith and for the assurance that nothing is impossible with You. Help me to keep my eyes fixed on You, even when the circumstances around me seem daunting or discouraging. Give me the strength to persevere in prayer and to trust in Your perfect plan for my life. In Jesus' name, Amen.

3. Holy Spirit, I invite You to minister to my heart and mind as I rest tonight. Help me to cast all my cares and concerns upon the Lord, knowing that He cares for me. Fill me with Your supernatural peace and joy, and remind me of Your constant presence and love. In Jesus' name, Amen.

4. Merciful God, I confess any areas of my life where I have allowed fear, stress, or anxiety to rob me of my faith and joy. I choose to surrender these burdens to You and to trust in Your unfailing love and faithfulness. Help me to find my rest and security in Christ alone. In Jesus' name, Amen.

5. Sovereign Lord, I declare Your sovereignty over my life and my body. I trust that You are in control of every detail and that Your plans for me are good. I choose

to submit to Your will and to trust in Your infinite wisdom, even when I cannot see the full picture. In Jesus' name, Amen.

6. Gracious Father, I pray for the blessing of godly mentors and examples who can encourage and inspire me in my journey of faith. Help me to learn from the testimony of others who have experienced the miracle of conception, and to find hope and strength in their stories. May I be a source of comfort and support to others who may be facing similar challenges. In Jesus' name, Amen.

7. Loving God, I thank You for the privilege of coming before Your throne of grace with confidence, knowing that You hear and answer my prayers. I trust that You are working behind the scenes on my behalf, even when I cannot see the evidence with my natural eyes. Help me to wait patiently on You, knowing that Your timing is perfect. In Jesus' name, Amen.

8. Holy Spirit, I ask that You would renew my mind and transform my thoughts to align with God's truth. Help me to meditate on what is pure, lovely, and praiseworthy, and to guard my heart against any negativity or discouragement. Fill me with Your hope and expectation for the miracle that is to come. In Jesus' name, Amen.

9. Merciful God, I lift up to You any feelings of shame, inadequacy, or unworthiness that may be hindering my faith for a miracle conception. I thank You that my identity and value are found in Christ alone, and that Your love for me is not based on my performance or ability. Help me to rest in Your unconditional love and acceptance. In Jesus' name, Amen.

10. Heavenly Father, as I lay down to sleep tonight, I entrust my body, my womb, and my future into Your

capable hands. I pray that You would watch over me and fill me with Your peace and presence. I declare that I will not fear, for You are with me; I will not be dismayed, for You are my God. You will strengthen me and help me; You will uphold me with Your righteous right hand. In Jesus' name, Amen.

## Prayers for Wisdom, Honor, and an Eternal Legacy
*Morning Prayers*

1. Heavenly Father, as I begin this day, I ask for a fresh infilling of Your divine wisdom. Like Mary, who pondered the events of her life in her heart, help me to seek understanding and insight from Your Holy Spirit. Grant me discernment to navigate the challenges and opportunities I face, and to make choices that honor You and align with Your will. In Jesus' name, Amen.

2. Gracious God, I pray that You would cultivate in me a heart of humility and a desire to serve others, just as Mary did throughout her life. Help me to find joy in putting the needs of Your Kingdom before my own, and to use the gifts and talents You have given me to bless and encourage those around me. May my life be a reflection of Your love and grace. In Jesus' name, Amen.

3. Sovereign Lord, I acknowledge that true wisdom comes from You alone. I pray that You would guide my steps and direct my path, helping me to make decisions that are pleasing in Your sight. When I am faced with difficult choices or uncertain circumstances, grant me clarity and peace to follow Your leading. In Jesus' name, Amen.

4. Loving Father, I pray that my life would bring honor and glory to Your name. Like Mary, who was chosen and favored by God, help me to live in a manner worthy of the calling I have received. May my words, actions, and attitudes reflect the character of Christ, and may

I be a light that points others to Your goodness and truth. In Jesus' name, Amen.

5. Holy Spirit, I ask that You would fill me with the wisdom and discernment I need to navigate the complexities of this world. Help me to see people and situations through Your eyes, and to respond with compassion, grace, and truth. When I am tempted to rely on my own understanding, remind me to trust in You and to seek Your guidance. In Jesus' name, Amen.

6. Merciful God, I confess that there are times when I struggle to make wise choices or to act in a manner that brings honor to Your name. Forgive me for the moments when I have allowed pride, selfishness, or fear to guide my decisions. Help me to repent and turn back to You, and to rely on Your strength to live a life of integrity and faithfulness. In Jesus' name, Amen.

7. Gracious Father, I pray that You would use my life to create an eternal legacy that points others to Christ. Like Mary, whose story has impacted countless generations, help me to live in a way that inspires and encourages others to follow You. May the fruit of my life be a testament to Your goodness and faithfulness, and may it bring glory to Your name long after I am gone. In Jesus' name, Amen.

8. Loving God, I thank You for the example of Mary, who willingly submitted to Your plan and purpose for her life. Help me to cultivate a heart of obedience and surrender, and to trust in Your wisdom and guidance, even when the path ahead is unclear. May my life be a living sacrifice, holy and pleasing in Your sight. In Jesus' name, Amen.

9. Holy Spirit, I ask that You would give me the wisdom and courage to speak truth and life into the world around me. Like Mary, who declared the goodness

and faithfulness of God through her song of praise, help me to proclaim Your truth with boldness and compassion. May my words bring hope, healing, and transformation to those who hear them. In Jesus' name, Amen.

10. Heavenly Father, I pray that You would establish the work of my hands and use my life to make a lasting impact for Your kingdom. Help me to invest my time, talents, and resources into things that have eternal value, and to store up treasures in heaven rather than on earth. May my legacy be one that points others to the hope and salvation found in Christ alone. In Jesus' name, Amen.

*Evening Prayers*

1. Gracious God, as I come to the end of this day, I thank You for the moments when Your wisdom and guidance were evident in my life. I praise You for the opportunities You gave me to honor You and serve others, and I trust that You will continue to lead me in the path of righteousness for Your name's sake. In Jesus' name, Amen.

2. Loving Father, I confess that there were times today when I struggled to make wise choices or to act in a manner that brought honor to Your name. I ask for Your forgiveness and cleansing, and I pray that You would help me to learn from my mistakes and to grow in my understanding of Your will. In Jesus' name, Amen.

3. Holy Spirit, I invite You to search my heart and reveal any areas of my life where I need to grow in wisdom, honor, or obedience. Help me to be open to Your conviction and correction, and to respond with repentance and humility. Give me the grace to let go of any attitudes or actions that do not align with Your

heart, and to embrace the transformation You desire to work in me. In Jesus' name, Amen.

4. Sovereign Lord, I declare that my life is in Your hands and that my future is secure in Christ. I trust that You are working all things together for my good and Your glory, and that the legacy of my life will be a reflection of Your faithfulness and love. Help me to rest in Your promises and to find peace in Your presence. In Jesus' name, Amen.

5. Merciful God, I lift up to You the areas of my life where I feel inadequate, unqualified, or unworthy. I thank You that my identity and value are found in Christ alone, and that Your strength is made perfect in my weakness. Help me to embrace the unique gifts and calling You have placed on my life, and to trust in Your ability to use me for Your purposes. In Jesus' name, Amen.

6. Gracious Father, I pray for the wisdom and discernment to navigate the relationships and responsibilities in my life. Help me to be a source of encouragement, support, and godly counsel to those around me, and to model the love and compassion of Christ in all my interactions. May my life be a testimony of Your goodness and grace. In Jesus' name, Amen.

7. Loving God, I thank You for the promise that Your Word will not return void, but will accomplish the purposes for which You have sent it. I pray that the seeds of truth and wisdom that have been planted in my life will take root and bear fruit, and that my legacy will be one that points others to the hope and salvation found in Christ. In Jesus' name, Amen.

8. Holy Spirit, I ask that You would fill me with Your peace and presence as I rest tonight. Help me to cast

all my cares and concerns upon You, knowing that You are able to guard my heart and mind in Christ Jesus. Give me the grace to let go of any worries or fears, and to trust in Your unfailing love and protection. In Jesus' name, Amen.

9. Merciful God, I lift up to You the areas of my life where I need healing, restoration, or breakthrough. I thank You that Your power is made perfect in my weakness, and that Your grace is sufficient for every need. Help me to trust in Your timing and Your methods, and to believe that You are working all things together for my ultimate good and Your glory. In Jesus' name, Amen.

10. Heavenly Father, as I lay down to sleep tonight, I entrust my life and my future into Your loving hands. I pray that You would watch over me and fill me with Your peace and presence. I declare that I will not fear, for You are with me; I will not be dismayed, for You are my God. You will strengthen me and help me; You will uphold me with Your righteous right hand. Thank You for the assurance that my life is hidden with Christ in You, and that my legacy will be one that endures for all eternity. In Jesus' name, Amen.

## Prayers to Expand the Kingdom of God and Pursue the Great Commission with Fervency

*Morning Prayers*

1. Heavenly Father, as I begin this day, I pray that You would ignite within me a passion for Your kingdom and a desire to see Your will be done on earth as it is in heaven. Like Mary, who dedicated her life to serving You and nurturing the Savior of the world, help me to prioritize Your purposes above my own and to use my time, talents, and resources to advance Your kingdom. In Jesus' name, Amen.

2. Gracious God, I thank You for the privilege of being

called as a laborer in Your harvest field. I pray that You would open my eyes to the opportunities around me to share the love and truth of Christ with those who are lost and hurting. Give me the boldness, wisdom, and compassion I need to be an effective witness for Your kingdom. In Jesus' name, Amen.

3. Holy Spirit, I ask that You would empower me to pursue the Great Commission with fervency and faithfulness. Help me to remember that the gospel is the power of God for salvation to everyone who believes, and that I have been entrusted with the ministry of reconciliation. May my life be a living testimony of the transforming power of Your grace and truth. In Jesus' name, Amen.

4. Loving Father, I pray that You would give me a heart of compassion for the lost and the marginalized, just as Jesus had compassion on the multitudes who were like sheep without a shepherd. Help me to see people through Your eyes, and to love them with the same sacrificial love that You have shown to me. May my life be a reflection of Your heart for the world. In Jesus' name, Amen.

5. Sovereign Lord, I acknowledge that the harvest is plentiful, but the laborers are few. I pray that You would raise up a new generation of disciples who are passionate about Your kingdom and committed to making Christ known in every sphere of society. Help me to be a mentor and encourager to those who are younger in the faith, and to invest my life in multiplying disciples for Your glory. In Jesus' name, Amen.

6. Merciful God, I confess that there are times when I am tempted to be complacent or apathetic about the Great Commission. Forgive me for the moments when

I have been more concerned about my own comfort or convenience than about the eternal destinies of those around me. Renew my zeal for Your kingdom, and help me to live with a sense of urgency and purpose. In Jesus' name, Amen.

7. Gracious Father, I pray that You would use my life to be a light in the darkness and a source of hope and healing to those who are broken and hurting. Help me to be sensitive to the needs of others and to respond with the love and compassion of Christ. May my words and actions point others to the truth of the gospel and the power of Your transforming grace. In Jesus' name, Amen.

8. Holy Spirit, I ask that You would give me the wisdom and discernment I need to navigate the challenges and opportunities of evangelism and discipleship in a complex and changing world. Help me to be creative and innovative in my approach, while remaining faithful to the timeless truths of Your Word. May I be a student of culture and a servant of Christ, always seeking to contextualize the gospel message in a way that is relevant and compelling to those I seek to reach. In Jesus' name, Amen.

9. Loving God, I thank You for the promise that Your Word will not return void, but will accomplish the purposes for which You have sent it. I pray that the seeds of the gospel that I sow in the lives of others will take root and bear fruit, and that many will come to know You as their Lord and Savior. Help me to trust in Your power to save and to never grow weary in doing good. In Jesus' name, Amen.

10. Heavenly Father, I pray that You would use my life to advance Your kingdom and to bring glory to Your name. Like Mary, who played a crucial role in the

redemptive story of God, help me to embrace the unique calling and purpose You have for my life. May I be a faithful steward of the gifts and opportunities You have given me, and may my life be a testament to the power of Your love and grace. In Jesus' name, Amen.

*Evening Prayers*

1. Gracious God, as I come to the end of this day, I thank You for the opportunities You gave me to be a witness for Your kingdom. I praise You for the conversations, the encounters, and the moments when I saw Your hand at work in the lives of others. I trust that You will continue to use my life to draw people to Yourself and to advance Your purposes in the world. In Jesus' name, Amen.

2. Loving Father, I confess that there were times today when I missed opportunities to share the love and truth of Christ with those around me. I ask for Your forgiveness and cleansing, and I pray that You would help me to be more attentive to the promptings of Your Spirit. Give me the courage and the compassion to step out in faith and to be a bold witness for Your kingdom. In Jesus' name, Amen.

3. Holy Spirit, I invite You to search my heart and reveal any areas of my life where I have become complacent or indifferent to the Great Commission. Help me to rekindle my passion for the lost and to live with a renewed sense of urgency and purpose. Give me the grace to let go of any distractions or excuses that hinder me from fully pursuing Your call on my life. In Jesus' name, Amen.

4. Sovereign Lord, I declare that the gospel is the power of God for salvation to everyone who believes, and that Your kingdom will advance in the earth. I trust that

You are working in the hearts and lives of those I have prayed for and shared with, and that Your Word will accomplish the purposes for which You have sent it. Help me to rest in Your sovereignty and to find peace in Your promises. In Jesus' name, Amen.

5. Merciful God, I lift up to You the areas of the world that are yet unreached with the gospel message. I pray that You would raise up laborers for the harvest and equip them with the resources and strategies they need to make Christ known among the nations. Help me to do my part in supporting and sending those who are called to cross-cultural missions, and to be a faithful intercessor for the global Church. In Jesus' name, Amen.

6. Gracious Father, I pray for the unity and witness of Your Church in the world. Help us to lay aside our differences and to come together in the common cause of making disciples of all nations. May our love for one another be a testimony to the transforming power of the gospel, and may our lives be a reflection of the hope and healing that is found in Christ alone. In Jesus' name, Amen.

7. Loving God, I thank You for the promise that one day every knee will bow and every tongue will confess that Jesus Christ is Lord. I pray that I will live my life in light of that glorious day, and that I will be found faithful in pursuing Your kingdom purposes until You return or call me home. Help me to fix my eyes on Jesus, the author and perfecter of my faith, and to run with perseverance the race that is set before me. In Jesus' name, Amen.

8. Holy Spirit, I ask that You would fill me afresh with Your power and presence as I rest tonight. Help me to cast all my cares and concerns upon You, knowing

that You are able to do exceedingly abundantly above all that I could ask or imagine. Give me the grace to surrender my dreams and desires to Your perfect will, and to trust in Your ability to use me for Your glory. In Jesus' name, Amen.

9. Merciful God, I lift up to You the people and places that are on my heart tonight - the friends, family members, and coworkers who need to know the love and truth of Christ. I pray that You would open their hearts to receive the gospel message, and that You would use me as a vessel of Your grace and truth in their lives. Help me to persevere in prayer and to never give up hope for their salvation. In Jesus' name, Amen.

10. Heavenly Father, as I lay down to sleep tonight, I entrust my life and my ministry into Your loving hands. I pray that You would watch over me and fill me with Your peace and presence. I declare that I will not grow weary in doing good, for in due season I will reap a harvest if I do not give up. Thank You for the privilege of being called as a laborer in Your harvest field, and for the assurance that my labor in the Lord is not in vain. May my life bring glory and honor to Your name, and may Your kingdom come, Your will be done, on earth as it is in heaven. In Jesus' name, Amen.

# CLOSING CHAPTER: EMBRACING OUR LEGACY, LIVING OUR DESTINY

As we come to the end of our journey through the lives of Sarah, Rebecca, Leah, Tamar, Ruth, Rahab, Bathsheba, and Mary, we find ourselves standing on holy ground. We have walked alongside these remarkable women, witnessing their struggles, their triumphs, and the undeniable hand of God working through their lives. Each of their stories has served as a powerful testament to God's faithfulness, His redemptive power, and His ability to use imperfect individuals to accomplish His perfect will.

**Reflecting on Our Journey**

Let us take a moment to reflect on the key lessons we've gleaned from each of these extraordinary women:

1. Sarah taught us about the power of faith and the importance of trusting in God's timing, even when His promises seem impossible to our human understanding.

2. Rebecca's story showcased God's intricate providence and the significance of seeking His guidance in every decision we make.

3. Leah's life unveiled the depths of God's love for

the brokenhearted and the transformative power of turning our focus to Him rather than seeking validation from others.

4. Tamar's courage reminded us that God sees and vindicates the oppressed, and that He can bring justice and purpose out of even the most challenging circumstances.

5. Rahab's story demonstrated that no one is beyond the reach of God's grace, and that He can use even the most unlikely individuals for His glory.

6. Ruth's unwavering loyalty and faith inspired us to cling to God as our ultimate Redeemer, trusting in His plan even when the future seems uncertain.

7. Bathsheba's journey from scandal to royalty revealed the depths of God's mercy and His ability to bring redemption and purpose out of our darkest moments.

8. Mary's obedience and surrender showed us the beauty of aligning our will with God's, even when His call seems daunting or impossible.

**Our Place in God's Continuing Story**

As we close this book, it's crucial to remember that these women's stories are not just historical accounts or moral lessons. They are part of the grand narrative of God's redemptive plan, a plan that continues to unfold today. We, too, are part of this story. Like these women, we are called to play our unique roles in God's ongoing work in the world.

Each of us, regardless of our past, our current circumstances, or how insignificant we may feel, has a God-ordained destiny. The same God who worked in the lives of Sarah, Rebecca, Leah, Tamar, Ruth, Rahab, Bathsheba, and Mary is working in our lives today. He is the unchanging God, faithful through all generations.

**Living Out Our Legacy**

So how do we live in light of this incredible legacy? Here are some key takeaways as we move forward:

1. Embrace Your Unique Story: Remember that God can use every aspect of your life - the triumphs and the trials, the joys and the sorrows - for His glory and purposes.
2. Trust in God's Timing: Like Sarah, we may face seasons of waiting. Hold fast to God's promises, knowing that His timing is perfect.
3. Seek God's Guidance: Follow Rebecca's example by seeking God's wisdom in every decision, big or small.
4. Find Your Worth in God: Let Leah's story remind you to seek your validation and love from God rather than from others.
5. Stand for Justice: Like Tamar, have the courage to stand up for what is right, trusting that God sees and will vindicate you.
6. Believe in Redemption: Rahab and Bathsheba's stories remind us that no one is beyond God's reach. Believe in His power to redeem and transform lives.
7. Demonstrate Radical Faith: Ruth's story challenges us to step out in faith, even when the path ahead is uncertain.
8. Surrender to God's Will: Like Mary, cultivate a heart that says "yes" to God's calling, even when it defies human logic.

**A Call to Action**

As we conclude, I want to challenge you to take what you've learned from these women and apply it to your life. Here are some practical steps you can take:

1. Reflect: Take time to journal about which woman's story resonated most with you and why. What specific

lessons can you apply to your current situation?

2. Pray: Use the prayers provided at the end of each chapter as a starting point for your own conversations with God. Call upon the God of Sarah, Rebecca, Leah, Tamar, Ruth, Rahab, Bathsheba, and Mary in your own life.

3. Study: Dive deeper into the Scriptures. Read and meditate on the full biblical accounts of these women's lives.

4. Share: Don't keep these stories to yourself. Share what you've learned with others - your friends, family, or small group.

5. Act: Identify one specific action you can take this week to live out the lessons you've learned. Perhaps it's stepping out in faith like Ruth, or standing for justice like Tamar.

Remember, you are part of a long line of faithful women who have played crucial roles in God's plan. Your story matters. Your faith matters. Your obedience matters.

**A Final Prayer**

Let us close with a prayer:

Heavenly Father,

We thank You for the lives of Sarah, Rebecca, Leah, Tamar, Ruth, Rahab, Bathsheba, and Mary. Thank You for preserving their stories and using them to teach, encourage, and inspire us. We are grateful for the ways You've spoken to us through their lives.

Lord, we pray that You would help us to live out the lessons we've learned. Give us the faith of Sarah, the wisdom of Rebecca, the perseverance of Leah, the courage of Tamar, the loyalty of Ruth, the transformative faith of Rahab, the redeemed heart of Bathsheba, and the obedience of Mary.

We ask that You would write our stories into Your grand

narrative. Use our lives, Lord, for Your glory. Help us to trust You in the waiting, to seek You in our decisions, to find our worth in You, to stand for what is right, to step out in faith, to believe in Your power to redeem, and to surrender our wills to Yours.

May we, like these women, play our part in bringing Your kingdom to earth. May our lives point others to You and may we leave a legacy of faith for generations to come.

In Jesus' name we pray, Amen.

As you close this book, remember that your story is still being written. May you walk forward with confidence, knowing that the God of Sarah, Rebecca, Leah, Tamar, Ruth, Rahab, Bathsheba, and Mary is your God too. He is faithful, He is good, and He is not finished with you yet. Go forth and live out your God-given destiny!